Josh Mclaverty-Williams

C000152451

GCSE
BITESIZE
revision

Check and test

Modern World History

Allan Todd
(Assistant Principal Examiner, Modern World History)

Published by BBC Educational Publishing,
BBC White City, 201 Wood Lane, London W12 7TS.

First published 2001

© Allan Todd/BBC Worldwide (Educational Publishing) 2001. All rights reserved.

ISBN: 0 563 54348 5

Illustrations © Philip Hood (page 8), Hardlines Ltd (pages 18, 65, 78 and 84)

Colour reproduction by Spectrum Colour, England

Printed and bound by Poligrafico Dehoniano, Italy

BBC

Contents

About GCSE Bitesize

- **GCSE Bitesize** is a revision service designed to help you achieve success in your exams. There are **books, television programmes** and a website at **www.bbc.co.uk/revision**.

- The service is called Bitesize because it breaks revision down into bite-sized chunks, making it easier for you to remember.

How to use this book

- This book explains and tests a **100 things you should know** to succeed in GCSE Modern World History. It provides:

  - the key information you need, in the 'Check the facts' section

  - questions to test your understanding, in the 'Test yourself' section.

- Use this book to check your understanding of GCSE Modern World History. If you can prove to yourself that you're confident with these key ideas, you'll know that you're on track with your learning.

- You can use this book to test yourself:

  - during your GCSE course

  - at the end of the course during revision.

- As you revise, you can use *Check and Test* in several ways:

  - as a summary of the essential information for each of the 100 topics

  - to check your revision progress: test yourself to find out the topics with which you are most confident

  - as a way to keep track and plan your time: you can aim to check and test a set number of topics each time you revise, knowing how many topics you need to cover in total and how much time you've got.

GCSE Bitesize revision materials

There's nothing like variety for making revision more interesting, and covering a topic from several different angles is an ideal way to make it stick in your head. There are lots of **GCSE Bitesize Revision** materials in different media, so take take your choice and make learning enjoyable.

GCSE Bitesize Revision: Modern World History is a book containing the key information and skills you need to revise, plus lots of tips and practice questions to help you get the best results. *GCSE Bitesize Revision: Modern World History ISBN: 0 563 46122 5*

The **GCSE Bitesize Revision: History website** provides even more explanation and practice to help you revise.

Website address: **www.bbc.co.uk/revision**

The History exam

There are two different papers for the Modern World History exam. One is based mainly on testing your knowledge (and may also include questions that involve the use of sources), the other deals mainly with sources *and* also requires you to use your knowledge.

Regardless of your Board or syllabus, your answers will be level-marked. This means that for each question there will be a marking scheme (normally with two or three levels). The examiner then has to decide which level your answer fits. This decision will be based on the quality – not the quantity – of your answer. This is why it is important to do what the question asks and, where appropriate, to select relevant facts from your own knowledge.

To get a high grade in GCSE Modern World History you have to do two things:

• show what you know

• show what you can do with what you know.

This book provides you with all the main facts for the various GCSE topics.

Always read the questions carefully to see exactly what they mean. If you are pressed for time, give shorter answers to all the questions rather than long answers to only the easy ones. In that way, you will gain more marks!

Good luck!

BBC GCSE Check and Test: History

Check the facts

- Before 1914, rivalry over colonies (known as the **Scramble for Africa**) and trade led to increasing tension and an **arms race** between the main countries of Europe. **Nationalism** was an important factor in this rivalry.

- Rivalry led to the formation of two opposing alliances: the **Triple Entente** (Allies), consisting of Britain, France and Russia, and the **Triple Alliance** (Central Powers), made up of Germany, Austria and Turkey.

- **Italy,** part of the Triple Alliance, stayed neutral in 1914 and joined the Triple Entente in 1915.

> **The final steps to war were triggered by the assassination of the archduke of Austria in Sarajevo in June 1914.**

1914

1918

- By August 1914, Germany and Austria had declared war on Russia and France.

- On 4 August 1914, Britain declared war on Germany, after German forces (following the **Schlieffen Plan**) invaded Belgium. The Schlieffen Plan had been drawn up to enable Germany to survive a two-front war by invading France through Belgium before Russia had time to mobilise its troops.

- The Plan failed because the Russian army mobilised quicker than expected. Also, Belgium put up unexpected resistance, which slowed the German advance into France.

- The **British Expeditionary Force** (BEF) joined French forces in a successful counter-attack at the River Marne. This stopped the Germans capturing Paris and forced them to retreat.

Test yourself

1 Which country is missing from the list of:
a) the Allies?
b) the Central Powers?

Allies (Triple Entente)	Central Powers (Triple Alliance)
Britain	Germany
France	Austria
	Italy (until 1915)

2 What was the purpose of Germany's Schlieffen Plan?

3 Why did the Schlieffen Plan fail in August 1914?

Check the facts

- After the **Battle of the Marne**, the Germans retreated to a line of trenches. Both sides then began a 'race to the sea' – each side wanted to be the first to capture the Channel ports.

- By November 1914, the line of trenches on the Western Front stretched over 470 km, from the North Sea to Switzerland.

> **The armies of both sides were equal in size and their weapons (machine guns and heavy artillery) were more defensive than offensive.**

- As a result, a situation of **stalemate** soon existed on the Western Front.

- The war (which many had thought would be 'over by Christmas') soon settled into a pattern of attacks on the enemy's lines of trenches.

- There were several major battles, including:

  1915 – Ypres
  1916 – Verdun
  1916 – Somme
  1917 – Passchendaele

- However, these battles failed to bring about a breakthrough, or even to gain much ground, despite the heavy casualties.

- New tactics and weapons (artillery barrages, gas, tanks, planes) failed to break the stalemate, because each side copied the other side.

- As a result, the First World War quickly became a **war of attrition**, in which each side tried to destroy more of the enemy than it lost itself.

Test yourself

1 What was the 'race to the sea'?

2 Why did new tactics and weapons fail to bring about a decisive breakthrough?

3 What do you understand by the term 'war of attrition'?

Warfare

BBC GCSE Check and Test: History

Check the facts

- There were four main types of trench. Behind the **frontline trenches** (from where attacks were made) were **support trenches** and, behind these, **reserve trenches**. The three types of trench were connected by **communications trenches**, which allowed troops and messages to move backwards and forwards.

> **The ground that separated the opposing trenches was known as No Man's Land.**

- Attacks were preceded by heavy artillery barrages, which sometimes lasted for days. Before an attack, whistles were blown and the troops were ordered to advance across No Man's Land to attack the enemy trenches. This was known as 'going over the top'.

- A typical British trench looked like the one below:

soldier sleeping in dug-out   sandbag parapet   barbed wire

soldier writing letter   duckboards (mud and water below)   firestep   soldier using periscope

Cross-section of a British frontline trench

- Well-constructed German trenches tended to give better protection from artillery barrages than British trenches.

- Conditions in the trenches soon became dreadful, as the heavy shelling destroyed drainage systems. This, combined with rain, soon turned the trenches and No Man's Land into a sea of mud. Human remains provided food for rats, which often bit the sleeping soldiers.

Warfare

www.bbc.co.uk/revision

191
191

- Soldiers in the trenches also suffered from frostbite in the winter and typhus-bearing lice. The lice were known as **chats** and had to be cracked off by fingernails or burning. This was time-consuming, and the talking that took place during the process soon became known as **chatting**. Other medical problems included **trench foot** and **gangrene**.

- The prolonged shelling, gas attacks and awful conditions led soldiers to suffer nervous breakdowns. At first, the soldiers were shot for desertion or refusal to obey orders under fire. Later, the condition became recognised as **shell-shock** and medical treatment was provided.

- The heavy shelling that preceded an attack was intended to destroy the barbed wire protecting the enemy's trenches. However, this usually failed to happen. In addition, soldiers attacked carrying heavy packs (about 25 kg) and many wounded soldiers drowned in the mud in the shell-craters that existed in No Man's Land.

- If soldiers survived the machine-gun fire and made it across No Man's Land, and managed to get through the barbed wire, they would have to engage in vicious hand-to-hand fighting.

Test yourself

1 The diagram below shows a typical trench system.

Name the types of trench labelled A and B.

2 What do you understand by the terms (i) 'going over the top' (ii) 'No Man's Land'?

3 Name two medical problems often suffered by troops in the trenches.

4 At the beginning of the war, what often happened to soldiers suffering from 'shell-shock'?

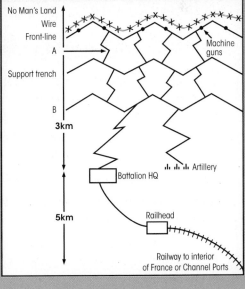

The First World War, 1914–1923

Check the facts

- Both sides used new tactics (such as prolonged heavy artillery barrages) to break the stalemate on the Western Front. However, these tactics failed and so new technology was used.

> **On land, some weapons (such as machine guns) actually led to a more defensive war. Other developments were:**

Gas: the first use of poison gas (chlorine) was by the Germans in 1915. Phosgene and mustard gas were later used by both sides. Despite early successes, the use of gas was dependent on the weather, so army commanders remained doubtful. Gas masks were developed to counter the effects.

191
191

Tanks: these were developed by the British Navy in 1915. They were first used in 1916 at the **Battle of the Somme**. Early problems included mud, heat and breakdowns. They played a more important role at the Battle of Cambrai in 1917, but were not fully used until 1918.

> **On sea, there were two main developments:**

Dreadnoughts: these were new larger and more powerful battleships, developed by both sides before 1914. However, they only fought one major battle (Jutland, 1916).

Submarines: the German **U-boats** destroyed much British shipping (25 per cent by April 1917) and were a serious threat.

> **In the air, there were also two main developments:**

Planes: at first, these were used for observation (scouting). Later, the invention of fixed machine guns, which fired through propellers, allowed the planes to attack enemy trenches. Aerial fights **(dog fights)** often took place. Planes were also used to bomb the trenches (at first, bombs were dropped by hand).

Airships: German Zeppelins bombed British towns and cities. They had poor navigation and found bad weather difficult.

Warfare

www.bbc.co.uk/revision

> Many of these inventions failed to produce the decisive breakthrough, as both sides made similar advances or copied the enemy. Also, the two sides developed ways of combatting the new technology.

- Britain countered German U-boats with:
  Hydrophones: these detected submarines, so that **depth charges** could then destroy the U-boats.
  A convoy system: this was even more effective. Merchant ships sailed together in **zig-zag patterns**, protected by destroyers and torpedo boats. By November 1918, British merchant shipping losses had dropped to 4 per cent.

- Britain dealt with Zeppelins by improving air defences. By 1916, Zeppelins were met with incendiary bullets, barrage balloons, searchlights and night fighters. Germany was forced to switch to **night bombers**.

Test yourself

1 What were the three types of poison gas used in the First World War?

2 Why were tanks not fully used before 1918?

3 What impact did German U-boats have?

4 How did Britain deal with the problems caused by U-boats?

5 Give two reasons why Zeppelins turned out to be ineffective.

The First World War, 1914–1923

Check the facts

On land, there were five other fronts, in addition to the Western Front:

1 On the **Eastern Front**, Austria–Hungary heavily defeated the Russians at Tannenberg and Mausarian Lakes in 1914. However, there was no trench warfare. Russia's **Brusilov Offensive** in June 1916 soon collapsed. By the end of 1916, German troops occupied large areas of Russia.

2 In the **Balkans**, there was heavy fighting during the Gallipoli Campaign (the Allies tried to capture the Dardanelles and so weaken Germany's ally, Turkey). In December 1915, the Allies were forced to withdraw. There was also fighting against Bulgaria in the Salonika Campaign.

3 The **Italian Front** saw bitter fighting between Italy (which switched to the Allies in 1915), Austria–Hungary and Germany. Italian losses were heavy at the battle of Caporetto in 1917.

4 In the **Middle East**, the Allies tried to protect oil supplies threatened by Turkey. The main fighting was in Mesopotamia (Iraq) and Palestine, where the Arabs revolted against Turkish rule.

5 In **East Africa**, the Allies quickly took Germany's colonies, although the war continued in East Africa until 1918.

There was also fighting at sea and in the air:

Sea

Britain and Germany both depended on importing food and materials. Protecting sea routes and merchant ships with a powerful navy was therefore vital. At first, German U-boats were a serious problem, but Britain soon imposed a naval blockade of all German ports.

Air

Aeroplanes were used against enemy trenches, while **dog fights** between opposing airforces also took place.

Test yourself

1 Which two countries fought against Russia on the Eastern Front?

2 What were the aims, respectively, of the Allied campaigns in: (i) Gallipoli (ii) the Middle East?

191
1918

Warfare

www.bbc.co.uk/revision

Check the facts

- During 1915 and 1916, despite new weapons, the stalemate at the Western Front continued.

- From March 1917, **revolution** in Russia weakened the war-effort of Britain and France's ally. However, in April 1917, the USA joined the Allies. Although US troops did not arrive immediately, Allied morale was boosted.

- Russia's involvement in the war was finally ended by the **Treaty of Brest–Litovsk** with Germany in March 1918. This treaty allowed Germany to switch most of its troops from the Eastern to the Western Front.

1914

1918

- Hindenberg and Ludendorff, the German commanders, decided to use these extra troops before US forces had time to build up. They were also worried about the effects of food shortages caused by Britain's naval blockade and the low morale of German soldiers and civilians. Their Spring (Ludendorff) Offensive **(Operation Michael)** used storm-troopers who had been specially trained and who were more mobile than regular troops.

> Germany's Spring Offensive **was at first successful and seemed to have ended the stalemate.**

- The Allies regrouped and, with extra US troops, **counter-attacked** in August. This counter-attack (with the first really effective use of tanks) soon began to push the Germans back. There were several factors behind this success: the Germans had attacked with no overall plan, and had no reserves and only limited supplies. Also, the German troops advanced so quickly that they tired themselves out. The Allies, on the other hand, had plenty of supplies and were reinforced with fresh US troops.

- With the threat of mutiny and revolution, Hindenberg and Ludendorff decided Germany would have to surrender. The **armistice** took effect on 11 November 1918.

Test yourself

1 What two important changes in the membership of the Triple Entente took place in 1917?

2 Why did the Germans decide to launch a massive surprise offensive in the spring of 1918?

3 Identify two reasons why this Spring (Ludendorff) Offensive failed.

Warfare

BBC GCSE Check and Test: History

The First World War, 1914–1923

Check the facts

- President Woodrow Wilson of the USA had issued his **Fourteen Points** in January 1918 as the basis of a **peace treaty** to end the war. The USA, with Britain and France (the **Big Three**), made most of the decisions about the peace treaties. The defeated members of the Central Powers were excluded from the talks.

> The **Big Three** had different aims. This caused problems when they met in January 1919.

- Britain was led by Lloyd George, who was re-elected in 1918. Many British people wanted Germany to be punished, and Lloyd George wanted to enlarge the British Empire by taking Germany's colonies. Overall, however, he wanted a **compromise peace**. This would prevent Germany seeking revenge. Germany would also be able to resume trade with Britain and would be kept strong enough to resist Communism.

- France, led by **Clemenceau**, wanted a **harsh peace**, as the country had suffered great destruction during the war.

> **Clemenceau wanted to make Germany weak by:**

- imposing huge compensation (reparations) for the damage and war debts
- taking large parts of German territory and industry
- forcing almost total disarmament.

- **Wilson** of the USA wanted a **just peace**.

> **Wilson wanted:**

- self-determination for all nationalities
- the setting up of a League of Nations to prevent future wars.

- Lloyd George and Clemenceau thought Wilson was too idealistic. Because Wilson was ill during the conferences and losing control of the US Congress, he was forced to make many concessions.

Test yourself

1 Which countries made up the Big Three at the peace conferences in 1919–20?

2 Who, respectively, were the leaders of (i) Britain (ii) France?

3 Why did France want to make Germany pay heavy compensation?

1919
192:

www.bbc.co.uk/revision

Check the facts

- There were many problems to solve when the Allies met in Paris in 1919, because (a) they disagreed and (b) the war had ended before serious discussions had taken place.

> **The biggest problem was Germany – it had almost single-handedly nearly won the war.**

- The Allies wanted to be sure that Germany would not be strong enough to fight another war. There was also political chaos in Germany, as workers' risings and mutinies in the armed forces (some inspired by the Bolshevik Revolution in Russia) had led the **kaiser** (emperor) to flee. It had also left the new government weak.

> **In central and eastern Europe, nationalism was breaking up the Austro–Hungarian empire.**

1919

1923

- This led to the formation of independent but weak countries (Poland, Czechoslovakia and Yugoslavia).

- In Hungary, a **communist revolution** broke out in March 1919.

- Large areas of Europe (especially Germany, where the Allied blockade remained in force) were suffering from **near starvation** and **economic collapse**. Millions died from a severe flu epidemic.

- Many – particularly in France and Belgium – wanted revenge on Germany for the human and economic costs of the war. Millions had been killed or horribly wounded, and many farms, factories, roads and railways had been destroyed.

- Other countries, such as Italy and Japan (as well as groups such as the Jews and Arabs), had been promised land in secret deals and now wanted their rewards. But some of these were **conflicting promises** or were **opposed** by Wilson.

Test yourself

1 Why was there political chaos in Germany at the end of 1918?

2 Which large central European empire was broken up by nationalist and communist uprisings?

3 What impact did the British naval blockade have on Germany?

BBC GCSE Check and Test: History

The Peace Treaties, 1919–23

Check the facts

- Five separate peace treaties were signed between the Allies and the members of the defeated Central Powers. The most important was the **Treaty of Versailles** with Germany in June 1919. Germany was not involved in the discussions and was given only days to agree to the treaty. If Germany refused, the war would begin again.

- All Germany's overseas colonies were taken and handed over to Britain, France or Japan under League of Nations' mandates.

In Europe:

Alsace–Lorraine was returned to France, which was also allowed to run the Saar (an important industrial area) for 15 years.
Upper Silesia and **Posen** went to Poland, which also gained West Prussia as a **corridor** to the sea. This split East Prussia from the rest of Germany.
Danzig became an International Free City, run by the League of Nations.
North Schleswig went to Denmark and **Eupen–Malmédy** to Belgium.
Anschluss (union) with Austria was forbidden.
The Rhineland (German land from the Rhine to France's border) became a demilitarised zone.

1919

1923

Germany's armed forces were reduced to keep the country weak, as follows:

- the army was limited to 100 000; conscription was banned
- tanks and military aircraft were forbidden
- the navy was reduced to six small battleships
- submarines were banned.

- Germany was also forced to sign a **War Guilt** clause (Article 231), accepting total responsibility for starting the war and agreeing to pay **reparations** (compensation). This was fixed at £6600 million in 1921.

- Finally, Germany was not allowed to join the League of Nations.

Test yourself

1 What happened to Germany's overseas colonies?

2 Name two parts of Germany's European territories lost as a result of the Treaty of Versailles.

3 What do you understand by the term 'Anschluss'?

Check the facts

- Because Germany was not given a chance to influence the terms of the Treaty of Versailles, it objected to the way in which the treaty was forced on the country – especially as the new government thought it would be based on Wilson's Fourteen Points.

> **Most Germans saw the treaty as a diktat (dictated peace).**

- Many Germans resented the loss of land, industry, population and their colonies. They also objected to the lack of self-determination for Germans and German-speakers in the new countries formed from the Austro–Hungarian empire. The ban on Anschluss with Austria was seen as especially unfair.

- They also disliked the military restrictions imposed on their armed forces and their exclusion from the League of Nations.

> **Many Germans felt resentment over the War Guilt clause and the amount of reparations.**

- Historians are divided over how unfair the treaty was. Those who see it as unfair, point to the fact that it was not based on Wilson's Fourteen Points, and that it punished the German people, who had had little influence over the kaiser and the military commanders.

- Others argue that Germany did not lose that much territory – and certainly far less than they took from Russia by the **Treaty of Brest–Litovsk** in 1918. They also point out how quickly the German economy recovered in the second half of the 1920s.

Test yourself

1 Why did many Germans see the Treaty of Versailles as a *diktat*?

2 What was the 'War Guilt' clause?

3 Why did so many Germans object to this?

919

923

BBC GCSE Check and Test: History

Check the facts

• Germany's defeated allies (Austria, Hungary, Bulgaria and Turkey) were dealt with by four separate treaties. The Austro-Hungarian empire was split into several separate countries (known as the **Successor States**). Austria and Hungary became two separate countries.

> **At first, Austria, Hungary, Bulgaria and Turkey were all banned from joining the League.**

• **Austria** was dealt with by the **Treaty of St Germain**, 1919. The South Tyrol and Istria went to Italy. Other areas went to Poland, Czechoslovakia and Yugoslavia. The Austrian army was reduced. **Anschluss** with Germany was forbidden.

• **Hungary** signed the **Treaty of Trianon**, 1920. Land was lost to Czechoslovakia, Yugoslavia and Romania. Its army was reduced.

• **Bulgaria** was dealt with by the **Treaty of Neuilly**, 1919. Land was lost to Yugoslavia, Greece and Romania. Its army was also reduced.

• **Turkey** signed the **Treaty of Sevres**, 1920. Its empire in the Middle East went to Britain and France (under League of Nations' mandates). Most of its European lands went to Greece; and it had to pay reparations to the Allies.

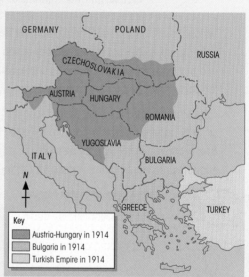

Key
- Austria–Hungary in 1914
- Bulgaria in 1914
- Turkish Empire in 1914

Test yourself

1 What happened to the Austro–Hungarian empire as a result of the Treaties of St Germain (1919) and Trianon (1920)?

2 What do you understand by the term 'Successor States'?

3 Name two of the Successor States.

The Peace Treaties, 1919–23

1919

192

The First World War, 1914–1923

Check the facts

- In general, the treaties added to the disruption of the economy of central and eastern Europe. This led to reduced trade after the war. Also, the **Successor States** contained many different national groups, some of whom did not want to be part of them. Theses states were also weak in military terms.

- In addition, many of the defeated countries were unhappy with the treaties. Because of a Communist uprising, a treaty wasn't signed with Hungary until 1920. The new **right-wing dictatorship** resented the loss of territory (about 60 per cent). In Turkey, the harsh **Treaty of Sevres** led to a nationalist revolt (led by Mustafa Kemal). Turkey then attacked Greece to take back lost land. The Allies agreed to return most of this in the **Treaty of Lausanne**, 1923.

Some of the Allies were unhappy with the treaties.

- Italy was angry that much of the land it had been promised by the secret Treaty of London, 1915, went to Yugoslavia.

- France felt Germany had not been weakened enough and needed reparations to pay off its war debts to the USA.

- Britain, however, thought the Treaty of Versailles had been too tough on Germany; it did not support France's hardline approach.

Test yourself

1 What were the economic results of the break-up of the Austro–Hungarian empire in central and eastern Europe?

2 Why was the Treaty of Trianon with Hungary delayed until 1920?

3 Who was Mustafa Kemal?

Check the facts

- Wilson's **Fourteen Points** included the setting up of a **League of Nations**. The first sections of all the peace treaties dealt with its establishment.

- The League of Nations' headquarters were in **Geneva** in neutral Switzerland. Membership was open to all but the defeated Central Powers, who were not allowed to join until they had proved their commitment to peaceful solutions. Communist Russia was also not allowed to join.

It was agreed that the League of Nations **should have three main aims:**

- to prevent war by reaching solutions to problems by negotiation
- to bring about disarmament
- to improve health, education and living and working conditions across the world through special commissions (poverty, inequality and injustice were thought to be important factors in causing wars).

The powers and methods open to the League to help prevent or end aggression were:

- pressure of world opinion
- economic sanctions (trade bans) by all member countries
- force, as a last resort.

The structure of the League of Nations

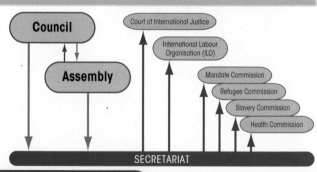

Test yourself

1 What document issued by Woodrow Wilson in 1918 set out his ideas for a League of Nations?

2 Identify the League's two main aims.

3 What did its special committees deal with?

4 What do you understand by the term 'sanctions'?

The League of Nations, 1919–39

Establishment of the League, 1919–20

www.bbc.co.uk/revision

Check the facts

- Despite the hopes surrounding the establishment of the League of Nations, it had many **weaknesses**. During the 1920s, and especially the 1930s, these weaknesses began to undermine its effectiveness.

> **One of the League's biggest problems concerned membership. Three of the most important countries in the world did not belong: the USA, Russia and Germany.**

- Although Wilson **(Democrat)** had pushed hard for the League to be set up, the idea was not popular in the USA. Wilson lost control of Congress to the **Republicans** in 1918. The Republicans then refused to accept US membership. Russia did not belong (because it had a Communist goverment), while Germany was prevented from joining as part of its punishment after the war.

- The League was thus dominated by **Britain** and **France**, so the defeated and excluded countries had little respect for its decisions. Instead, they saw it as a **victors' club** or (in the case of Russia) a **capitalists' club**.

> **Countries such as Japan resented the fact that the League was totally dominated by white European countries.**

- The League was further weakened by the fact that Britain and France did not agree on what should happen in Europe, and so did not always cooperate. Britain was much more interested in its empire and did not want to see France dominate Europe. France, on the other hand, wanted to prevent Germany becoming economically and militarily strong again.

Test yourself

1 Why was the USA's non-membership of the League of Nations a problem?

2 Why was the fact that the League depended on Britain and France a serious weakness?

The League of Nations, 1919–39

Check the facts

The League of Nations was able to settle several disputes between countries in the 1920s. These included:

1921: Upper Silesia, between Poland and Germany
1921: Aaland Islands, between Finland and Sweden
1925: Greece's invasion of Bulgaria.

- The League's attempts to achieve lasting peace through disarmament were less successful, although there were some postive results. Attempts to draw up a disarmament treaty were blocked by Britain in 1923. In 1926, Germany was allowed to join the League.

- There were other steps towards peace and disarmament. These tended to be a result of direct diplomacy or the work of the Conference of Ambassadors, rather than the efforts of the League. However, the League had done much to create the atmosphere in which such agreements could be made.

The League contributed to the following agreements being made:

- 1922: the **Washington Treaty**, between the USA, Britain, France and Japan (limiting naval expansion for ten years)
- 1925: the **Locarno Pact**, in which Germany accepted its western borders as drawn by the Treaty of Versailles, and agreed that any changes to its eastern borders should be by discussion
- 1928: the **Kellogg–Briand Pact**, whereby 45 countries agreed never to resort to war as a way of resolving disputes.

- The League also did much good work through its special commissions. In particular, many refugees from the war were helped to return home. It also tried to stop slave labour and the use of dangerous chemicals, while its Health Committee reduced disease across the world.

1919

1939

Test yourself

1 Name two successes that the League of Nations had in dealing with disputes in the 1920s.

2 What progress did the League make towards disarmament in the 1920s?

3 Apart from disputes and disarmament, in what other areas did the League have a degree of success during the 1920s?

The League in action, 1919–39

Check the facts

**The League had several failures in the 1920s.
The most important ones were:**

1920–21: **Russo–Polish War.** The League failed to prevent this war. In fact, its two most important members, Britain and France, backed Poland.

1921:   **Vilna**, between Poland and Lithuania. The Polish army seized this disputed town in 1921. The League failed to get Poland to withdraw and to allow the inhabitants to vote. The dispute was finally settled by the Conference of Ambassadors, which gave the town to Poland.

1923:   **The Ruhr**, which was invaded by France and Belgium when Germany failed to make its second reparations payment. Although France was a leading member of the League, this occupation was carried out without informing the League.

1923:   **Corfu**, which involved Italy's seizure of this Greek island after an Italian boundary official was killed by an unknown gunman while working for the Conference of Ambassadors on the Greek–Albanian border. Mussolini invaded Corfu and demanded massive compensation. Italy, an important member of the League, ignored the League's attempts to mediate. The problem was finally settled by the Conference of Ambassadors, which ordered Greece to pay 50 million lire to Italy as compensation.

- In all these cases, the League had been unable to stop aggression by strong countries. In two cases, the aggression had been committed by important members of the League. As a result, at the end of the 1920s, people were beginning to criticise the League's inability to prevent or end aggression.

- An attempt at signing a disarmament treaty in 1923 failed, when proposals were blocked by Britain.

Test yourself

1 How was the dispute over Vilna solved?

2 How did the occupation of the Ruhr in 1923 show the weakness of the League?

3 What important failure, involving Italy, did the League have in 1923?

The League in action, 1919–39

919

939

BBC GCSE Check and Test: History

Check the facts

- Despite successes in the 1920s, the League had not established itself as the main body for settling disputes. Its most important members often followed **different policies**. Nonetheless, the League still achieved success in the 1930s:

  1932: a border dispute between Colombia and Peru was settled by the League

  1934: the Soviet Union became a member of the League.

- However, the League was weakened by the impact of the Great Depression, which followed the **Wall Street Crash** in 1929. As a result, many countries (including Italy, Japan and Germany) came to be ruled by extreme nationalist governments that adopted aggresssive foreign policies to solve their economic problems.

- Many other countries put their own economic interests first. They were therefore reluctant to impose economic sanctions on an aggressive country in case it harmed their own trade. They included non-members, such as the USA, as well as members, such as Britain and France.

- By the mid-1930s, many felt the League was unable to prevent aggression because of its weaknesses. The main problems were:

  – the absence of the USA

  – its close identification with the victors of the First World War and the peace treaties

  – the lack of unity between Britain and France

  – the lack of its own armed forces to act against aggression and impose solutions.

Test yourself

1 What success, involving two minor non-European countries, did the League have in 1932?

2 What was significant about this success, in light of the League's growing problems?

3 Why did the Great Depression make it more difficult for the League to settle disputes in the 1930s?

191

193

Check the facts

The League suffered three main failures before 1936. These were:

1 **Manchuria:** Manchuria was a Chinese province. Both Japan and China were League members. In September 1931, Japan invaded Manchuria. The League ordered Japan to withdraw. The Japanese government agreed, but the army refused.

In December 1931, the League set up the **Lytton Commission** to investigate. By February 1932, all of Manchuria had been occupied by the Japanese and was renamed 'Manchukuo'. The Lytton Report, November 1932, ordered Japan to withdraw. The Report was accepted by the League but, in February 1933, Japan simply left the League.

2 **World Disarmament Conference:** this Conference lasted from 1932–3 and was a continuation of the failed attempt in 1923. However, Hitler became **chancellor** (prime minister) of Germany in 1933. He demanded **equality of treatment** – either all countries should disarm to the level imposed on Germany in 1919 or Germany should be allowed to match the levels of other countries. Agreement could not be reached, and Hitler took Germany out of the Conference and the League.

3 **Abyssinia:** in October 1935, Fascist Italy invaded Abyssinia. Because Britain and France saw Italy as an ally against Germany, no real action was taken. The Suez Canal was not closed to Italian supply ships. Oil, coal and steel were not in the trade sanctions imposed by the League. Non-members, such as the USA and Nazi Germany, continued to trade with Italy.

Instead of opposing Italy, Britain and France drew up the secret **Hoare–Laval Pact**, which would give two-thirds of Abyssinia to Italy. However, the pact collapsed and, in December 1936, the League finally placed sanctions on oil and petrol. But it was too late – in May 1936, Italy renamed Abyssinia '**Ethiopia**'. Although the League ended all sanctions in July 1936, Italy left the League in December 1937.

Test yourself

1 Why did the Disarmament Conference in 1933 fail?

2 How did the invasions of Manchuria and Abyssinia show up the weaknesses of the League?

The League of Nations, 1919–39

Check the facts

- Russia was ruled by a **Tsar** (emperor) who had absolute power, i.e. there was no democracy. Most of the land was owned by a few **noble families**. Over 80 per cent of the population were poor, illiterate peasants.

- **Industrialisation** had begun in the 1890s as a result of foreign investment. The factories were large and conditions were poor. After 1900, an industrial depresssion and bad harvests led to wage cuts, unemployment and high food prices.

- In 1904, the Tsar, Nicholas II, declared war on Japan. The Russo–Japanese War went badly for Russia. A peaceful Russian demonstration in January 1905 was fired on by soldiers and this **Bloody Sunday** sparked off the **1905 Revolution**

- At first, those who wanted change united against the Tsar. They included the **Kadets** (middle-class liberals), the **Social Revolutionaries** (mainly supported by peasants) and the **Social Democrats** (a Marxist party, which, in 1903, had split into Menshevik and Bolshevik factions).

> The Tsar issued the October Manifesto. It promised a Duma (parliament) and free speech.

- The Kadets ended their opposition and the Tsar used the army to crush the workers and their **soviet** (strike committee), which had been set up in St Petersburg.

- The Tsar then went back on his promise, giving little power to the Duma. Elections were organised to give greater representation to the rich. The Tsar dismissed the Duma's criticism of his actions and ordered new elections. By 1912, he was back to ruling without a parliament.

Test yourself

1 Name one factor that led to the 1905 revolution.

2 What was the October Manifesto of 1905?

3 How did Nicholas II break his promises in the years before 1914?

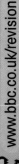

1917

1924

Check the facts

- After the **1905 Revolution**, the Tsar's new chief minister, Stolypin, carried out a **harsh repression** in which many involved in the revolution were hanged. As well as reducing opposition, Stolypin also began **land reform** to win the support of those peasants who were better off. In 1911, Stolypin was **assassinated**.

> **In the years 1911–14, protests and strikes began to increase in Russia.**

917

- In 1914, in an attempt to stop the protests, Nicholas II decided to become involved in the First World War. A series of defeats led him to take command of the army in 1915. However, while he was at the front, the government came under the control of **Rasputin**. The war soon resulted in food and fuel shortages in the towns, which led to protests and strikes. Poor leadership and lack of equipment and clothing led to **mutinies** in the army.

924

- Suffering was made worse by the harsh winter of 1916–17.

> **In March 1917, protests by women in Petrograd (St Petersburg) grew into the March Revolution.**

- The police lost control, and many soldiers joined the demonstrators. On 15 March 1917, Nicholas II abdicated.

- A Provisional Government (temporary and unelected) was set up by members of the Duma. At the same time, workers and soldiers elected the Petrograd Soviet, reviving the one formed in 1905. This was at first dominated by the Social Revolutionaries **(SRs)** and the Mensheviks, who both supported the Provisional Government.

- From March to November 1917, a situation of **Dual Power** existed – the Soviet's Order No. 1 said workers and soldiers should obey the Provisional Government's orders provided they agreed with Soviet decisions.

Test yourself

1 How had Stolypin tried to win the support of peasants?

2 Name one factor which sparked off the March Revolution in 1917.

3 What do you understand by the term 'Dual Power'?

Check the facts

Lenin and Revolution, 1917–24

- The unelected Provisional Government, led by Prince Lvov, immediately released **political prisoners** and granted **free speech**. Free elections for a proper parliament were promised, but no date was set.

- Its other decisions were less popular: Russia should stay in the war, and no reforms should be carried out until after the war. Peasants and workers began occupying land and factories, while elected soviets were set up all over Russia.

- Revolutionary unrest increased after April, when **Lenin** (leader of the **Bolsheviks**) returned from exile. His **April Theses** encouraged workers and peasants to take action.

> **Lenin's two slogans were 'Peace, Bread and Land' and 'All Power to the Soviets'**

191

192

- At first, not all Bolshevik leaders agreed, as the Bolsheviks were only a minority in the soviets.

- In May 1917, **Trotsky** returned to Russia. Although he had sided with the Mensheviks in 1903, since 1904 he had been an independent. Trotsky now decided to join the Bolsheviks, as his and Lenin's ideas had become similar. It wasn't long before Trotsky became an important Bolshevik spokesperson.

- As the war and food and fuel shortages continued, the Bolsheviks began to win more seats in the soviets. Then, in July 1917, soldiers and workers tried to overthrow the Provisional Government, now led by **Kerensky** (a former SR). Although the Bolsheviks had not planned the **July Days**, Kerensky banned the Bolsheviks and arrested their leaders. Lenin escaped to Finland.

- An attempted coup in September by **Kornilov** (Commander-in-Chief) caused Kerensky to panic.

> **Kerensky released the Bolsheviks and gave weapons to their Red Guards.**

- The **coup collapsed**, and the Bolsheviks' increased popularity resulted in them winning majorities for the first time in many soviet and city council elections.

www.bbc.co.uk/revision

- Lenin decided the time had come for a second revolution to overthrow Kerensky. Some Bolsheviks were opposed, and their Central Committee finally voted 10 to 2 in favour. Because Lenin was still a wanted man, the main organisation for the revolution was done by Trotsky, recently elected as chair of the Soviet's **Military Revolutionary Committttee** (MRC).

> **On 6–7 November, Bolshevik Red Guards and**
> **MRC soldiers overthrew Kerensky in**
> **the November Revolution.**

- Power passed to the All-Russian Congress of Soviets, which had just opened and had a Bolshevik majority. It elected a government (Sovnarkom), with **Lenin** as Chairman (prime minister). **Trotsky** became Commissar for Foreign Affairs. The less well-known **Stalin** was appointed Commissar for Nationalities.

- All land was taken from the nobles, but the Peasants' Congress rejected the Bolshevik idea of nationalising the land. The All-Russian Congress also voted for an immediate end to the war and for self-determination for all nationalities.

- In December 1917, the SRs split into Left and Right, with the Left joining the Bolsheviks in a **coalition**. News of this did not reach rural areas until elections to a new **Constituent Assembly** had taken place (Kerensky had set the date just before he was overthrown). The Bolsheviks won 175 seats to the Right SR's 370. Even with the 40 Left SRs, it meant the new government was in a minority.

Test yourself

1 What were the two main slogans of Lenin's 'April Theses'?

2 What elected body shared power with the unelected Provisional Government?

3 Who planned most of the practical details for the Bolshevik November Revolution?

4 Which political group formed a coalition with the Bolsheviks in December 1917?

917

924

Russia in Revolution, 1917–41

Check the facts

- The Constituent Assembly met in January 1918, but was immediately closed down, as the Kadets and other groups who were opposed to the November Revolution threatened counter-revolution. The **Cheka** was set up to deal with these threats.

The biggest problem was ending the war.

- Many peasant soldiers were deserting to share out the nobles' land, and large parts of Russia were occupied by German troops. Lenin wanted an immediate peace, but others in the government disagreed.

In the Treaty of Brest–Litovsk, signed in March 1918, Germany forced Russia to give up much land and resources.

1917

- The Left SRs left the coalition in protest.
- By then, a **Civil War** had broken out between **Reds** (Communists) and **Whites** (anti-Communists). Several Allied armies also intervened on the side of the Whites. Both sides resorted to terror at times – with a **'Red Terror'** countering the **'White Terror'**.

1924

- The Reds seemed likely to lose, as the Whites had several well-equipped armies and controlled most of Russia. The Communists had just their **Red Guards** and controlled only the central parts of Russia. Trotsky, as Commissar of War, used **conscription** and many ex-Tsarist officers to quickly build up a large and efficient **Red Army**.
- The Reds were united, and their control of the centre – containing the main railways and factories – allowed them to move troops and supplies quickly from one front to another. The Whites' leaders often refused to cooperate with each other. In addition, many peasants didn't want a White victory, as the landlords would take back their land. Many others disliked foreign intervention.
- By 1920, the Whites were on the verge of total defeat when Poland invaded Russia. The Whites were defeated, but Poland was victorious.

The Russo-Polish war was ended by the Treaty of Riga in 1921, which took much Russian land.

Test yourself

1 What treaty ended Russia's involvement in the First World War?
2 Give one reason why the Reds won the Civil War.

Check the facts

- Although the Communists wanted state-owned farms, they thought factories would still have to be run by their private owners (**state capitalism**). However, peasants took over the land for themselves, while workers occupied factories and placed them under workers' control.

> **When the Civil War began, the Communists introduced emergency economic measures known as War Communism.**

- This included the government **nationalising** (taking over) all factories, ending private trade and forcing peasants to sell surplus food at a fixed price to feed the Red Army and factory workers.

- As the Civil War progressed, the Communists also began to restrict soviet democracy by limiting elections and banning certain political groups.

- Many factory workers – especially the anarcho-syndicalists – resented central control, while most peasants objected to the low prices. The peasants began to grow less food and to hide any surplus. The government sent in armed requistion squads to seize the grain.

- This, plus the disruption caused by the Civil War, led to **starvation** in several parts of Russia by 1921. So, Lenin suggested a change of policy. At first, this was rejected by most Communists.

> **The Kronstadt Rebellion took place in March 1921. Sailors and workers in Kronstadt rose in revolt against War Communism.**

- They were led mainly by anarchist groups, who also demanded a return to full democracy in the soviets. Trotsky was ordered to crush the revolt. This resulted in the deaths of thousands of Red Army soldiers and rebels.

Test yourself

1 Why was 'War Communism' introduced?

2 How did the peasants react to the government's plans to take their surplus grain production?

Check the facts

- The Kronstadt Rebellion persuaded the Communist government to accept Lenin's earlier proposals to change economic policy. This was the **New Economic Plan** (NEP), which replaced **War Communism**.

> **NEP was controversial as it involved a partial return to capitalism (the private sale of consumer goods and food, and small factories being returned to former owners or leased out for profit).**

- Some Communists called it the **New Exploitation of the Proletariat**. However, the government kept control of the 'commanding heights' of the economy: the banks, railways, heavy industry and foreign trade.

- In agriculture, peasants paid their taxes in food and were allowed to sell surplus food for profit. Peasants who increased production had their tax reduced.

- Because NEP involved a limited revival of capitalism, the Communist Party decided, as a temporary emergency measure, to ban other parties from the soviets and factions in their own party.

- By 1924, NEP had achieved some success – agricultural production had increased and industry was back to pre-war levels. However, the **kulaks** (rich peasants) and **nepmen** (private traders) were becoming very wealthy, and this worried many Communists.

Table of production figures, Russia, 1913–26

	1913	1921	1922	1923	1925	1926
Grain (million tonnes)	80	37	50	57	73	77
Cattle (millions)	59		46		62	
Pigs (millions)	20		12		22	

New Economic Policy's production figures

Test yourself

1 Why were some Communists opposed to Lenin's NEP?

2 What were (i) *kulaks* (ii) *nepmen*?

Lenin and Revolution, 1917–24

www.bbc.co.uk/revision

Check the facts

**In 1922, Stalin became General
Secretary of the Communist Party.**

- This job partly involved appointing and dismissing party officials and admitting or expelling members.

- Soon, however, some of Stalin's actions began to worry Lenin and other Communists such as Trotsky. One concern was the new **federal constitution** he drew up for the USSR. Although each national group had its own republic, Stalin gave great powers to central government.

- In 1922, Lenin suffered the first of several strokes, which kept him out of active politics for most of the time. Lenin's growing worries led him to turn to Trotsky in an attempt to restore party democracy.

- Although popular with the Red Army and ordinary party members, Trotsky had few friends among the party leaders. Many – such as Zinoviev, Kamenev, Bukharin and especially Stalin – resented his sudden rise in the party and his closeness to Lenin. Trotsky also became ill during this period.

**Lenin wrote his Testament in December 1922, outlining the
strengths and weaknesses of the main Communist leaders.**

- Lenin later added a 'Postscript', which recommended that Stalin be dismissed from all positions of power. Then, in 1924, Lenin died.

- Stalin used jealousies between the party leaders, Trotsky's illness and his powers as General Secretary to stage-manage Lenin's funeral to make it seem as though he had been very close to him. Stalin then persuaded the party leaders (despite the protests of Lenin's widow) not to act on or publish the *Testament*.

Test yourself

1 What important party job did Stalin get in 1922?

2 What did Lenin say about Stalin in the Postscript to his 'Testament'?

917

924

Stalin and the Soviet Union, 1924–41

Check the facts

- Zinoviev and Kamenev (both more popular than Stalin) thought they could use Stalin to stop Trotsky becoming the new party leader.

> **Zinoviev, Kamenev and Stalin formed the Triumvirate.**

- The first stage in Stalin's rise involved defeating Trotsky. Pre-1917 disagreements with Lenin were published and a one-sided debate over policy took place. Trotsky continued to defend the policy of **Permanent Revolution**. Lenin and other leaders – as well as Trotsky – argued that backward Russia would never be able to achieve socialism on its own, so it was necessary to help workers' revolutions throughout the world. It would also involve large-scale **industrialisation** and moves to large **state-owned farms**.

- Stalin, however, developed his idea of **Socialism in One Country**. This said Russia could achieve socialism on its own. This more conservative and gradual policy appealed to many ordinary party members.

- By using his position as General Secretary, and the 1921 ban on factions, Stalin got the party to outvote Trotsky. In 1925, Trotsky was forced to resign as Commissar of War.

- In the second stage, Stalin turned on Zinoviev and Kamenev, who were beginning to have doubts about Stalin's policies and motives. When they formed the **United Left Opposition** with Trotsky, Stalin accused them of **Trotskyism**. Supported by the Centre and Right of the party, Stalin had Zinoviev and Kamenev expelled from the party in 1927.

> **The final stage involved Stalin defeating the Right, who were led by Bukharin.**

- In 1928, Stalin suddenly decided to end NEP, but Bukharin and the Right disagreed. Stalin began to dismiss Bukharin's supporters. In desperation, Bukharin turned to Trotsky in an attempt to restore democracy. But it was too late. Bukharin was defeated in 1929 and Trotsky was expelled from the USSR. This left Stalin as sole leader of the Communist Party.

192

194

Test yourself

1 From what potentially powerful position was Trotsky forced to resign in 1925?

2 What was the United Left Opposition?

3 Why did Stalin and Bukharin fall out in 1928?

www.bbc.co.uk/revision

Check the facts

- Stalin's plans to modernise Soviet industry needed a more efficient agricultural system. Peasants would have to produce more food to feed the extra factory workers. Surplus food would be exported to buy more advanced foreign machinery.

- Most farms were small and used old-fashioned farming methods. Many poorer peasants had no land at all.

- In 1927, peasants were encouraged to join their plots to form larger state collective farms **(kolkhozes)** that would be more efficient. However, few did – the **kulaks** were especially keen to keep their privately-owned farms.

> **A food shortage in 1928 led Stalin to begin compulsory collectivisation.**

- Most of the land given to peasants in 1917 became state collectives, with peasants only allowed small private plots. The government then set up **Motor Tractor Stations** (MTS) to provide tractors and other modern machinery to make collectives more efficient.

> **There was much opposition to collectivisation, especially from the kulaks.**

- Many slaughtered their animals and destroyed crops and machinery, rather than turn them over to the collectives. In some areas, Communist officials were attacked and killed.

- Stalin then resorted to harsh measures. Many were hanged, and many more were sent to poor farming areas or to the **gulags** (prison work camps). Those who remained were reluctant to work hard.

- Food production dropped sharply, so the government sent armed detachments into the countryside to collect food for the towns. In some rural areas, several million people died from famine. It was not until 1941 that production levels returned to those of 1928.

Test yourself

1 What was a *kolkhoz*?

2 How did the *kulaks* react to forced collectivisation?

Check the facts

- Despite the success of the NEP, the USSR had only limited industry. In 1928, Stalin decided on rapid industrialiation, as he feared invasion by capitalist countries.

> **Since their intervention in the Civil War, capitalist countries had maintained an economic blockade against Soviet Russia.**

- Stalin also saw industrialisation as a way of breaking the influence of the wealthy **nepmen** and **kulaks**, thus allowing him to make the USSR more socialist. So, all factories that under NEP had been privately owned were now nationalised.

- The State Planning Commission (Gosplan) drew up a **Five-Year Plan** that set targets for increased production for each industry. Each factory and, eventually, each worker was given a **production target**.

- The **First** Five-Year Plan (1928–32) concentrated on heavy industry (coal, iron, steel, oil and electricity).

- The **Second** Five-Year Plan (1932–7) was similar to the First, but also developed **transport and mining**.

- The **Third** Five-Year Plan, which began in 1938, put more emphasis on **light industry, housing** and **consumer goods** (it later switched to war production because of the growing threat from Nazi Germany).

- Overall, despite official exaggeration and the failure to meet targets, these **Five-Year Plans** were successful in achieving spectacular increases in industrial production.

> **Many new industries and industrial centres were built. This enabled the USSR to withstand and then defeat the Nazi invasion in 1941.**

- By 1940, the USSR was the world's second largest industrial producer, after the USA.

	1927	1930	1932	1935	1937	1940
Coal (million tonnes)	36	61	65	102	130	152
Steel (million tonnes)	3	5	6	13	18	18
Oil (million tonnes)	12	17	21	24	26	26
Electricity (million kWh)	18	22	20	45	80	90

Table of industrial output, 1927–40. Compiled from Soviet and Western sources by an economic historian

192

194

- Stalin used many methods to achieve increased production. Skilled foreign workers were employed to teach new techniques. Workers who exceeded their work 'norms' received extra pay, various privileges and medals. These 'super' workers were known as 'Stakhanovites', after the miner **Stakhanov**, who had greatly increased his output.

> **Women and peasants were also encouraged to work in factories. Free crèches and canteens were provided to make it easier for women to work.**

- However, some of the methods were harsh. Hours of work were increased, fines for lateness were imposed and many were sent to the gulags, where they had to work in poor conditions.

- Although the Plans were successful, 'real' wages fell at first. There were also shortages of housing and consumer goods in the early years. But there were also benefits: no unemployment, free health care and free education (unlike most capitalist countries in the Depression of the 1930s). In the mid-1930s, things began to improve.

Test yourself

1 Give one reason why Stalin decided to modernise Soviet industry after 1928.

2 What do you understand by the term 'heavy industry'?

3 By how much did coal production increase between 1927 and 1940?

Russia in Revolution, 1917–41

Check the facts

- Although Stalin had defeated all his rivals by 1929, he still feared opposition. Even his supporters had been reluctant to expel leading Communists. He therefore expanded the **secret police** (renamed NKVD in 1934) to spy on possible critics.

- In 1934, Kirov (party boss in Leningrad) was assassinated. He had been very popular at the Seventeenth Party Congress earlier that year.

> **Stalin used the death of Kirov as an excuse to launch the Great Purge and Terror.**

- Thousands of party officials were arrested. In a series of Show Trials (1936, 1937 and 1938), many former leading Communists were accused of plotting against the Soviet Union. Most were condemned to death and executed, while others committed suicide. The victims included Zinoviev, Kamenev and Bukharin. Trotsky was sentenced to death in his absence, and was assassinated in Mexico in 1940.

- In 1937, Stalin extended the Great Purge to the armed forces. By 1939, about 20 per cent of all officers had been executed, including over half of the most senior ranks. Soon, even technical experts and factory managers were being arrested. Many were sent to the **gulag** camps, run by the NKVD – the conditions and food were so bad that they often died there.

> **Stalin also used propaganda and a personality cult to show himself as the true heir to Lenin and the only man capable of defending the USSR.**

- Statues and posters of Stalin appeared everywhere, and films and books praised his actions. He also took control of the **Komsomol** (Young Communist League).

192

194

Test yourself

1 Who was Kirov?

2 What were the Show Trials?

3 How did the Great Purge and Terror affect the armed forces?

Check the facts

- After the **November Revolution** in 1917, fourteen different countries had intervened in the Civil War on the side of the Whites.

> **In 1919, in an attempt to help spread world revolution and end Russia's isolation, the Communists set up the Communist International (Comintern).**

- However, under Stalin and his policy of **Socialism in One Country**, the Comintern declined in importance.
- During the 1920s, Germany was the only country prepared to deal with Russia. Treaties signed in 1922 and 1930 gave Russia modern technology in return for carrying out military training of German soldiers in Russia.
- After the **Wall Street Crash** in 1929, Stalin feared European capitalist countries might try to solve their problems by invading the USSR. In 1932, he signed a non-aggression pact with France. Japanese aggression against China in the Far East was another worry.

924

> **Stalin's security concerns increased after 1933, when Hitler came to power in Germany.**

- Stalin's concerns grew because Hitler intended to take **Living Space** for Germany from eastern Europe, and especially from the Soviet Union.
- At first, Stalin tried to get agreements with Britain and France. In 1934, the USSR was allowed to join the League of Nations. The Comintern was ordered to form **Popular Fronts** with all those opposed to fascism.
- However, Stalin became alarmed at Britain and France's policy of appeasing Hitler's demands and at Hitler's breach of the Treaty of Versailles, especially after the Czech Crisis over the Sudetenland in 1938.

941

- Stalin – in view of Britain and France's continued refusal to sign an anti-Nazi agreement – decided to buy extra time for the USSR by signing a Non-Aggression (Ribbentrop–Molotov) Pact with Germany in August 1939. This **Nazi-Soviet Pact** contained secret clauses to divide Poland between them, providing the USSR with a buffer zone. The Pact would also give the USSR time to build up its defences.

Test yourself

1 Why did Stalin's fears about Soviet security increase after 1933?
2 Give one reason why Stalin agreed to the Nazi-Soviet Non-Aggression Pact of August 1939.

Check the facts

Weimar Germany, 1919–33

By 1918, Germany was in a desperate state.

- Germany's army was defeated, the Allied naval blockade was creating near-starvation conditions, there were serious fuel shortages and the country was in financial ruin.

- In October 1918, sailors at Kiel mutinied. Soon, workers and soldiers in Kiel and elsewhere began to form councils and soviets. As mutinies and uprisings spread across Germany, the **kaiser** (emperor) fled and abdicated.

- Germany had not been a full democracy under the kaiser. The powers of parliament had been limited and free speech restricted. Once the kaiser had gone, a provisional government was set up under the leadership of Ebert, a leading member of the **Social Democratic Party** (SPD).

Ebert declared Germany a democratic republic, agreed to sign an armistice with the Allies and arranged for elections in January 1919.

- However, in Berlin, the revolutionary socialists of the Spartacist League tried to start a **workers' revolution** similar to the one that had taken place in Russia in November 1917.

- Ebert, under pressure from army leaders, agreed to call in the army to crush this **Spartacist Revolt**. Unemployed right-wing soldiers (the **Freikorps**) were also used to put down the rising.

- Thousands of workers were killed during the suppression. These included the leaders, Karl Liebnechkt and Rosa Luxembourg, who were captured and then murdered. Those who survived later formed the German Communist Party (KPD) and remained bitterly opposed to the SPD for what they saw as treachery.

191

193

Test yourself

1 What do you understand by the term 'Freikorps'?

2 What happened to the Spartacist leaders?

Check the facts

- The Spartacist Revolt and its suppression in Berlin forced the provisional government to move to Weimar to draw up a new democratic constitution for Germany. This is why Germany from 1919–33 is often referred to as the **Weimar Republic**.

> The new **Weimar Constitution** gave the vote to all over the age of 20 and used a system of proportional representation (PR) for elections to the **Reichstag** (parliament).

- Elections were to take place every four years. Governments – headed by a **chancellor** (prime minister) – were chosen from, and were responsible to, the Reichstag.

> Germany became a **federal system**, with power shared between central government and eighteen new **Länder** (state) governments.

- Article 48 of the constitution gave the president emergency powers to rule by decree without the Reichstag, and even to suspend the constitution. The president was to be directly elected every seven years.

- Because of PR, there were many small parties in the Reichstag, so most Weimar governments were often short-lived coalitions. From 1919–23, Germany had nine coalition governments. This was at a time when many Germans were bitterly angry at the Treaty of Versailles. Many blamed the new government for signing it and referred to them as the **November Criminals**, who had 'stabbed Germany in the back'.

- The constitution also had a **Fundamental Rights** section, which guaranteed several basic human and citizens' rights, including **free speech**, **religious beliefs** and the **right to travel freely**.

Test yourself

1 What powers did Article 48 of the Weimar Constitution give to the president?

2 Why were there often coalition governments in the Weimar period?

Weimar Germany, 1919–33

BBC GCSE Check and Test: History

Check the facts

> **The new Weimar Republic faced a number of problems.**

- There were many Germans who hated the Weimar Republic for signing the armistice and the Treaty of Versailles. Also, most of the civil servants, judges and army and police officers who had served under the kaiser kept their jobs after 1918 – many of them were opposed to democracy.

> **There was much violent political opposition to the Weimar Republic from both the Left and the Right.**

- The extreme Right carried out numerous murders of left-wing and liberal politicians in the years 1920–23.
- In March 1919, the new **Communist Party** organised strikes in Berlin. These were suppressed by the army and the Freikorps. There was also a Communist uprising in Munich, in which the army shot many workers.

> **In March 1920, the army made no effort to stop Kapp's Putsch (an attempted Freikorps coup against the government).**

- The putsch was defeated by a general strike organised by Berlin's workers. This then led to a **Communist uprising** in the Ruhr, which was bloodily suppressed by the army and Freikorps.
- Over two thousand workers were shot in the Communist uprising of 1920.
- There were also economic problems. In 1922, Germany said it could not afford to pay its second reparations instalment. So, in 1923, French and Belgian troops occupied the Ruhr (Germany's main industrial area). This was done without Britain's support.
- Germany replied with **passive resistance** (strikes and non-cooperation). The French deported 150 000 strikers and 132 Germans were killed in separate incidents.
- The German economy collapsed, leading to hyper-inflation (massive and rapid price increases) that even began to affect France. A new German government, led by Stresemann, ended passive resistance and the French finally withdrew.

191

193

Test yourself

1 What action did the army take against Kapp's Putsch in 1920?
2 Why did France invade the Ruhr in 1923?

Check the facts

- In 1919, **Adolf Hitler** (an Austrian who had fought in the German army) was sent to Munich to spy on the small **German Workers' Party** (DAP).

- Hitler joined this party. In 1920, it became the NSDAP **(Nazi Party)** and adopted a 25-Point Programme that contained nationalist and anti-Semitic (anti-Jewish) policies, with some vague socialist elements.

> **In 1921, Hitler became leader of the Nazi Party and adopted the swastika as the party emblem.**

- Hitler was a powerful public speaker, and blamed all Germany's problems on the Weimar Republic, Communists and Jews.

- He set up the Stormtroopers (SA). These **'Brownshirts'** (so-called because of their uniform) were mainly unemployed ex-soldiers who attacked left-wing political meetings and demonstrations. The Nazis soon had over 50 000 members in southern Germany.

- German nationalists were furious when passive resistance against the French occupation of the Ruhr was called off. Hitler decided to march to Berlin to overthrow the Weimar government.

- In November 1923, the Nazis took over a beer hall where important Bavarian officials were addressing a meeting. Hitler tried unsuccessfully to get their suppport for his **March on Berlin**.

- However, Hitler – supported by General Ludendorff (a First World War leader) – went ahead with his plans. But his **Beer Hall Putsch** collapsed, when the march was stopped by armed police. In the fighting, one policeman and sixteen Nazis were killed.

> **Hitler ran away and was later arrested.**

- Hitler was accused of treason, but the Munich judges allowed him to make long speeches that were widely reported across Germany by sympathetic newspapers. He was given the lightest possible sentence – five years in Landsberg prison.

Test yourself

1 When did Hitler become leader of the Nazi Party?

2 What were the Stormtroopers?

3 When did Hitler attempt his 'Beer Hall Putsch'?

919

933

BBC GCSE Check and Test: History

Check the facts

- The 1923 **hyperinflation** in Germany caused great hardship for many – especially those with savings or on fixed incomes (e.g. pensioners). Money became so worthless that workers were paid twice a day so that items could be bought before prices went up again.

- In September 1923, Gustav **Stresemann** became chancellor. He called off passive resistance and promised to pay reparations. In November, he introduced a new currency (the Rentenmark) to end inflation. German industry began to revive and unemployment fell. He then began to restore Germany's position by cooperating with the Allies.

- In 1924, Stresemann negotiated the **Dawes Plan** with the USA.

> The **Dawes Plan** **reduced the size of reparation instalments and provided Germany with US loans to modernise and build new factories.**

- In 1929, the **Young Plan** brought more loans, while reparations were reduced and spread over 60 years. Between 1924–9, Germany received over 25 billion gold marks in loans – three times more than the reparation payments. By 1929, Germany was second only to the USA in advanced industrial production.

- Stresemann also improved Germany's diplomatic position. In 1925, he signed the **Locarno Treaty**, which accepted Germany's 1919 western frontiers and stated that changes in the East would only be by negotiation. In 1926, Germany was allowed to join the League of Nations. In 1928, the **Kellogg–Briand Pact** saw Germany, along with 44 other countries, **renounce war**. These agreements led to greater foreign investment in German industries.

191

193

Test yourself

1 How did Stresemann deal with the hyperinflation of 1923?

2 What did the Dawes Plan (1924) and the Young Plan (1929) do about Germany's reparation payments?

Check the facts

- Stresemann's policies led to the **Golden Years** of the Weimar Republic in the years 1924–9. They achieved some of the policies demanded by the Right. As a result, support for extreme parties declined.

- Although Hitler had been sentenced to five years for his part in the **Beer Hall Putsch**, he was released in December 1924 after serving only nine months.

> **While in prison, Hitler had written Mein Kampf, which set out his ideas and plans.**

- Hitler's ideas and plans were a mixture of nationalism and racism, along with a hatred of Communism and democracy.

- However, when Hitler was released from prison, he found Germany much improved. He also found that the Nazi Party had been banned, was split into factions and membership had dropped. As a result, the Nazis did badly in elections in the years 1924–30. This period is known as the Nazis' **Lean Years**.

- Hitler reorganised the party. It was relaunched in 1925, with power concentrated in his hands. Special sections were set up to recruit more members (e.g. students, teachers, farmers and the **Hitler Youth** for young people) and party branches were set up all over Germany. In 1926, **Goebbels** took control of **propaganda**.

> **By 1928, the Nazis had just over 100 000 members.**

- Hitler also decided that in order to win power, the Nazis would have to use elections. The experience of the Beer Hall Putsch convinced him of the need to win over the army and wealthy industrialists.

- However, Hitler had no intention of abandoning violence and in, 1925, he set up the blackshirted **SS** (Schutz Staffel). Officially, this was his personal bodyguard, but it soon increased in size and attacked opponents. In 1929, **Himmler** became head of the SS.

Test yourself

1 What book did Hitler write while in Landsberg Prison?

2 Why did the Nazi Party need to be relaunched in 1925?

3 Who were the SS?

Check the facts

- In 1929, Stresemann died. Shortly after, the **Wall Street Crash** in the USA ended US loans and previous loans had to be paid back. This quickly showed the weaknesses of the German economy, which had been dependent on US loans to revive industry and help farmers.

> The Great Depression **soon affected most of the world and trade fell sharply.**

- In Germany, unemployment rose rapidly from under a million in 1928 to over 6 million by 1932. Those with jobs suffered from reduced hours and wage cuts. Soon millions were hungry and even homeless.

- In March 1930, the coalition government collapsed because of **policy differences**. President Hindenburg (elected 1925) appointed Bruning of the Centre Party as chancellor. When Bruning failed to get majority support in the Reichstag, he increasingly resorted to **rule by decree**.

- This political confusion, and the economic crisis, led many conservative Germans (who had never supported the Weimar Republic) to turn to extreme **right-wing** parties.

> The Nazis blamed all problems on the Communists **and** Jews, **and promised to make Germany great again.**

- In September 1930, the Nazis' Reichstag seats increased from 12 to 107. At the same time, more and more workers began to support the KPD (German Communist Party). In 1930, the KDP won 77 seats.

- The growth of the Communists worried wealthy industrialists. Many gave funds to the Nazis after Hitler made it clear his party was not really socialist.

- These huge sums of money allowed the Nazis to buy up eight newspapers, enabling them to spread their ideas more widely. The money also financed massive propaganda in the 1932 elections. In the April presidential election, Hitler won 13 million votes to Hindenberg's 19 million.

> In the July 1932 elections, the Nazis **became the biggest party, with 230 seats.**

191

193

- The Nazi rise was also helped by the violence of the SA (Stormtroopers), who, in 1932, numbered about 500 000. As well as weakening the Nazis' opponents, the violence made it look as though the Weimar Republic could not keep law and order. The huge military-style Nazi processions made Hitler seem the only man capable of restoring order.

- Continued rivalry between the parties led to a frequent change of government. In the November 1932 elections, the Nazis remained the largest party but lost 34 seats, while the Communists rose again.

Table of number of seats won by parties in elections in Germany, 1928–32

	1928	1930	1932 July	1932 Nov
Nazis	12	107	230	196
German Nationalist Party (DNVP)	73	41	37	52
German People's Party (DVP)	45	30	7	11
Centre Party	62	68	75	70
German Democratic Party (DDP)	25	20	4	2
Social Democratic Party (SPD)	153	143	133	121
Communists	54	77	89	100
Other	67	91	33	32
Total	491	577	608	584

Results of the elections to the Reichstag, 1928–32

- In January 1933, von Papen (leader of the Nationalists) persuaded Hindenburg to appoint Hitler as chancellor of a Nationalist-dominated coalition government.

Test yourself

1 Why did the Wall Street Crash have such a strong impact on Germany?

2 When, according to the chart, did the Nazis become the largest party in the Reichstag?

3 When did Hitler become chancellor of Germany?

Germany, 1918–45

Check the facts

- Although there were only three Nazi ministers in his government, Hitler planned to have complete power. He quickly called an election for March 1933. The SA and SS increased their violence against the KPD (German Communist Party) and the SPD (Social Democratic Party).

> **In February 1933, just before the elections, the Reichstag Fire took place.**

- The Nazis blamed the fire on the Communists. Their leaders and candidates were quickly rounded up.

- In Prussia (the largest of the **Länder**, or states), the Minister of the Interior was Goering, a leading Nazi. He enrolled SA members into the police and moved against the KPD and SPD. Over four thousand people were arrested. Their meetings were broken up and newspapers banned.

- The Nazis failed to get an overall majority in the Reichstag, despite banning those Communists who had managed to get elected.

> **The Nationalists then agreed to support the Nazis. This gave Hitler control.**

- Hitler got the Reichstag to pass the **Enabling Act** in March 1933 by intimidating and excluding SPD deputies. Hindenburg agreed to suspend the constitution and gave Hitler the power to rule by decree for four years. Hitler then moved quickly to destroy Weimar democracy.

- In April 1933, all eighteen Länder were taken over by Nazi **gauleiters**. In May, trade unions were banned. In July, all opposition parties were banned (or persuaded to disband) and Germany became a one-party dictatorship. By then, most KPD and SPD leaders and activists were in concentration camps run by the SA.

> **By early 1934, Germany was under Nazi control, but Hitler faced opposition from the more militant wing of the SA, including its leader, Ernst Rohm.**

- The militant wing of the SA wanted Hitler to carry out the left-wing promises of the Party Programme and for the SA to become the new German army. However, the army officers and the industrialists were opposed.

193

194

- In June 1934, Hitler ordered the **Night of the Long Knives**, in which the SS (with army help) murdered Rohm and other SA leaders. This reassured the generals and, when Hindenburg died in August, they supported Hitler in becoming **Führer of Germany.** Hitler was now **president**, **chancellor** and **C-in-C** of the armed forces.

> **The Nazi dictatorship was then maintained through terror.**

- The **Gestapo** (secret police) and the SS (which, by 1935, had risen to over 200 000) – both controlled by Himmler – used **informers**, about 400 000 **Block Leaders** (Nazi supporters who supervised blocks of flats) and mass arrests to intimidate potential opponents.

- After 1934, the SS took over the running of concentration camps – by 1939, there were six.

> **At first, the concentration camps were mainly for political prisoners (Communists, Socialists and trade unionists), but later they also took Jews, criminals, those who tried to avoid regular work and gays and lesbians.**

- The Nazis also made skilful use of censorship and propaganda to isolate opponents and build support. This was directed by **Goebbels** as Minister of Propaganda and Culture.

- Cheap radios were produced, and loudspeakers were placed in all work places and public areas to ensure everyone heard Nazi views. Newspapers were either banned or censored and had to print stories in line with Nazi policies.

- The Nazis' massive **Nuremberg Rallies** were filmed for the cinema, which also reflected Nazi ideas. Works of literature and art that conflicted with Nazi ideas were outlawed and destroyed.

Test yourself

1 Why was the Enabling Act of March 1933 so important in the Nazi plan to destroy the Weimar Republic?

2 What happened as a result of the 'Night of the Long Knives' in June 1934?

3 What government job did Goebbels have in 1933?

933

945

Germany, 1918–45

39 The Nazi economy

The Nazi Dictatorship, 1933–45

Check the facts

- Hitler was more interested in foreign policy but realised he needed to strengthen the economy. He decided to reduce unemployment, make Germany self-sufficient and rearm.

> **The Nazis dealt with unemployment in several ways.**

- The National Labour Service (set up before 1933) was expanded. From 1935, labour service (where all men were conscripted to carry out public works) was compulsory for all men aged 18–25 for six months.

- Public works – funded by government money – also gave work to the unemployed. The main projects were building houses, hospitals, schools, roads (to allow quick movement of troops) and barracks. Communists, those in concentration camps and Jews and women forced out of jobs were not counted as unemployed. By 1939, unemployment had fallen to 100 000 from over six million in 1932 (see page 46).

- The drive for **self-sufficiency**, closely linked to Hitler's plans for war, also created new jobs. Under Schacht, Minister of the Economy, agricultural production was increased, imports were reduced and attempts were made to find substitutes for foreign goods.

> **Rearmament began in secret in 1933 but, by 1935, was carried out openly.**

193

- Rearmament gave employment to many, as did the introduction of **conscription**. In 1936, Goering was ordered to get Germany ready for war. Goering's Four-Year Plan undermined Schacht's work and Schacht resigned in 1937.

194

- When **trade unions** were abolished in 1933, all workers had to join the Nazis' **German Labour Front**. Strikes were illegal, wages remained low (even after full employment) and the hours of work rose. To keep workers happy, various schemes (such as **Strength through Joy**) were developed to provide cheap holidays and leisure activities.

Test yourself

1 Identify one way in which the Nazis tried to reduce unemployment after 1933.

2 What was the idea behind Goering's Four-Year Plan of 1936?

www.bbc.co.uk/revision

Check the facts

- Nazi policies for women were based on the '3 Ks' **(Kinder, Kirche, Kücher)**. Women were encouraged to stay at home and have children by a system of loans. The **Motherhood Cross** system gave medals to women who had large families. Women classed as 'unfit' were compulsorily sterilised.

- To make sure they stayed at home, laws forced women out of various state and professional jobs (civil service, education, law and medicine).

- Employers were encouraged to give all jobs to men. Most of the advances made by women under the Weimar Republic were removed. The Nazis even tried to control the appearance of women (make-up, trousers and hair-dye were discouraged).

> **The Nazis wanted to control young people to ensure support in the future. Boys were seen as especially important.**

- 'Unreliable' (i.e. anti-Nazi or Jewish) teachers were sacked. Those who remained had to swear loyalty to Hitler and join the Nazi **Teachers' League**. A new national curriculum was drawn up and centrally imposed.

1933

- Great emphasis was placed on **History** (to show the 'greatness' of the Nazis), **Biology** (to teach 'race science', which stressed the superiority of Aryans, or non-Jews) and **PE** (to get boys fit for the army and girls fit to be mothers).

- Out of school, young people were encouraged to join the **Hitler Youth** movements. There were separate groups for boys and girls and the different age-groups. In 1936, it became compulsory to join.

1945

Test yourself

1 Identify one method used by the Nazis to get women to stay at home.

2 What was the 'race science' taught in schools after 1933?

Check the facts

- The Nazis were racist and believed all non-Aryan groups were inferior: Jews, blacks, Slavs and gypsies (Sinti and Roma). Their obsession with racial 'purity' led to compulsory sterilisation and to euthanasia of the disabled.

> **The main victims of Nazi racism were Jewish people.**

- In 1933, Hitler ordered the SA and SS to organise a boycott of Jewish shops. Laws were passed to sack Jews from the civil service, the law and education. In 1934, Jews were banned from public facilities, such as parks and swimming pools.

- In 1935, the **Nuremburg Laws** removed German citizenship from all Jews and forbade inter-marriage. After 1936, other laws further restricted the rights of Jews to work or own property.

- In November 1938, Kristallnacht **(Night of Broken Glass)** saw attacks on Jewish homes, shops and synagogues after a Nazi diplomat had been assassinated by a Jew in Paris. About a hundred Jews were killed and over 20 000 were put in concentration camps. After a week of terror, the Nazis fined the Jews one billion marks.

> **After 1939, all Jews in countries invaded by Nazi Germany were forced to live in ghettos.**

- In summer 1941, Himmler ordered the SS to form **Special Action Groups** to kill all Soviet Jews. Then, at the Wannsee Conference in January 1942, it was decided to exterminate all Jews in Europe. This was called the **Final Solution**.

- **Extermination camps** (e.g. Auschwitz) were built in eastern Europe. About 6 million Jews died in this **Holocaust**. Another 5 million 'racially inferior' people were also murdered (Slavs, gypsies and homosexuals).

Test yourself

1 Which laws in 1935 removed citizenship rights from German Jews and forbade inter-marriage between Aryans and Jews?

2 What was decided at the Wannsee Conference in January 1942?

1933

1945

Check the facts

- Many Germans (who were not Jewish, Communist or Socialist) supported the Nazis' policies on unemployment, rearmament and foreign expansion. However, in March 1933, even after intimidation and violence, the Nazis had only been able to win 43 per cent of the vote. There were many who continued to oppose Hitler's regime after 1933, despite Nazi propaganda and terror – even though most of them lost their lives doing so.

> **Communists and Social Democrats set up underground organisations that published anti-Nazi leaflets and organised industrial sabotage and strikes.**

- Many young people refused to join the Hitler Youth movements. Instead, they joined rebel groups – such as the Swing, the Meuten or the Edelweiss Pirates. University students in Munich formed the **White Rose Group**. They distributed leaflets, wrote anti-Nazi slogans on walls and even organised demonstrations. Their leaders were guillotined in 1944.

- Opposition even appeared in the army – especially when Germany began to do badly in the war. The most famous example was the failed July Bomb Plot in 1944, which tried to assassinate Hitler.

- There was also opposition from religious groups. Hitler was forced to drop his **euthanasia** programme because of protests from the churches.

- Upper-class Germans, who had at first supported the Nazis because of their anti-Communism, became alienated by Nazi corruption and brutality.

- When heavy Allied bombing, food rationing and hardships began to hit civilians, support for the Nazis declined even further. However, many Germans retained faith in Hitler himself.

Test yourself

1 Name one anti-Nazi youth group.

2 What did the White Rose Group do?

The Republican era: Boom and Bust, 1919–32

Check the facts

- The First World War (in which 100 000 US soldiers had died) ended in 1918. However, Woodrow Wilson, the Democratic president of the USA, wanted to continue US involvement in Europe. In fact, as early as 1918, he had drawn up his **Fourteen Points** as the basis for peace.

> **Many Americans – including some Democrats – wanted the USA to return to its traditional policy of isolationism, i.e. staying out of foreign alliances and avoiding close involvement in European affairs.**

- The US Congress, which had been dominated by Republicans since the 1918 mid-term elections, refused to sign the Treaty of Versailles or join the League of Nations.

- Before 1919, most immigrants to the USA had been White Anglo-Saxon Protestants **(WASPs)** from the more prosperous parts of northern and western Europe.

- By 1919, many Americans saw Europe as being full of poverty, oppression and dangerous revolutionary ideas and movements (e.g. socialism, communism and anarchism).

- After 1919, most immigrants to the USA came from the poorer parts of southern and eastern Europe – where there were many Catholics, and where many revolutionary outbreaks took place in the years 1917–20.

- The result was increasing restrictions on immigration, including the imposition of a literacy test in 1917 and limits and quotas in 1921, 1924 and 1929.

> **Between 1920 and 1929, immigration had fallen from 850 000 a year to 150 000.**

191

193

Test yourself

1 Which US political party did Woodrow Wilson lead?

2 When did the Republicans win control of the US Congress?

3 Who were the 'WASPs'?

www.bbc.co.uk/revision

The USA, 1919–45

Check the facts

- By 1918, the USA had become the most powerful industrial country in the world, with plenty of raw materials (wood, coal, iron, oil). It had stayed out of the First World War until 1917, and during that time had taken trade from European nations such as Britain and Germany.

> **US companies had made huge profits selling weapons to the Allies, while US banks had loaned money.**

- At the end of the war, these profits were invested in new industries (chemicals, cars, radios, electrical goods).

- Republican presidents, who ruled from 1920–29, believed in **laissez-faire** economics, i.e. lifting restrictions and taxes placed on US companies by Wilson to protect the public from the power of the larger firms and companies. The huge **trusts** (large firms) were now allowed to do as they wished. To help protect them from European competition, **tariffs** (customs duties) were imposed (e.g. the Fordney–McCumber Act, 1922).

> **New ways of producing, selling and buying consumer goods also increased sales and profits (mass production, radio advertising, hire purchase).**

- New industries, such as car manufacture, led to increased demand for steel, leather, glass and rubber and to massive road-building.

- Soon, **skyscrapers** dominated city skylines and the US economy experienced a boom as the number of cars, lorries, cinemas, department stores and clubs rose (the **Jazz Age**).

- For the first time, the majority of Americans lived in urban areas. However, many rural areas missed out on the prosperity of the 1920s, as did some groups of people (Black Americans, the poor and less wealthy farmers).

Test yourself

1 What do you understand by the term 'laissez-faire'?

2 Which industry symbolised the boom of the 1920s and helped stimulate other industries?

The Republican era: Boom and Bust, 1919–32

BBC GCSE Check and Test: History

The Republican era: Boom and Bust, 1919–32

Check the facts

- In 1918, women in the Anti-Saloon League and the Women's Christian Temperance Union succeeded in getting Congress to add the **Eighteenth Amendment** to the **US Constitution**. This made the sale, production and transport of alcohol illegal, while the **Volstead Act** in 1919 made buying alcohol illegal.

- These two women's groups (mainly rural) had pushed for such changes to avoid the problems associated with excessive alcohol consumption: poverty, absence from work, public drunkenness, crime and violence in the home and on the streets.

- Many US citizens were prepared to break the law to drink alcohol. This resulted in **speakeasies** (illegal bars), **moonshine** (illegally-made alcohol) and **bootlegging** (smuggling alcohol).

> **These developments gave new opportunities for organised crime and helped lead to the emergence of gangsters such as Al Capone and 'Bugs' Moran.**

- The gangs became so wealthy from supplying illegal alcohol that they were able to get involved in other crimes (prostitution, protection, gambling). They then used this wealth to bribe police, judges and local politicians. Capone was able to 'run' Chicago for several years (he was finally imprisoned in 1931 for tax evasion).

- As rival gangs fought to control areas, there was a huge increase in gang murders – the worst case was the **St Valentine's Day Massacre** in Chicago, 1929.

- The fighting increased crime and corruption. In 1933, the **Twenty-first Amendment** ended Prohibition.

1919

1933

Test yourself

1 Why did some groups campaign for the prohibition of alcohol?

2 What were 'speakeasies'?

3 Why was Prohibition ended in 1933?

www.bbc.co.uk/revision

Check the facts

- Black Americans suffered most from intolerance during the 1920s, as well as benefitting least from the boom. By 1920, there were 12 million blacks, of whom 75 per cent lived in the southern states where they experienced poverty and discrimination. Despite being freed from slavery in 1865, the **Jim Crow** laws in the southern states prevented most from voting and imposed segregation.

> **Black Americans suffered from Ku Klux Klan (KKK) violence, which included burnings, beatings and lynchings.**

- The **KKK** (an anti-black group set up in the South after the Civil War) had been revived in 1915.

- By 1925, the KKK had almost 5 million (WASP) members – including many law officials.

- During the 1920s, over 1.5 million blacks left the South for northern cities. Although there wasn't segregation in the North, they still experienced discrimination over housing, jobs and wages. There was also racial hostility and violence in some areas.

- Left-wingers and radicals were victims of a **Red Scare** during the 1920s. This scare was started by powerful Americans who were opposed to ideas of socialism, communism and anarchism.

- Left-wingers were harassed by the police and even deported from the USA. Wealthy industrialists, such as **Henry Ford**, refused to allow their workers to join trade unions, and even employed thugs against trade unionists and strikers.

- The most serious example of this intolerance was the case of two Italian anarchists, Sacco and Vanzetti, who were executed in 1927.

Test yourself

1 What do the initials 'KKK' stand for?

2 What was the 'Red Scare'?

Check the facts

- The US economy had several weaknesses, despite the 1920s boom:

  – Sixty per cent of the families were below the poverty line and so could not afford to buy consumer goods (the big trusts kept wages low).

  – Many who bought such goods had bought on HP (hire purchase).

  – The richest people (5 per cent owned 33 per cent of US wealth) had soon bought all they needed.

  – US industry found it difficult to export when other countries put tariffs on US goods in retaliation against US tariffs.

  – Competition from Australia and Argentina, and the increased use of cars and synthetic fabrics, led to reduced sales and overproduction. Prices fell; many farmers were evicted, while many farm workers lost their jobs.

- This over-production was made more dangerous by a boom in share prices, which encouraged millions of people to buy shares. By 1929, over 20 million owned shares, compared to 4 million in 1920.

- Many **speculators** bought their shares 'on the margin', while ordinary people bought them on HP. Others (by illegal evasion, known as **skulduggery**) bought up sufficient shares to control many industries.

> **In autumn 1929, investors lost confidence in the US economy and began panic-selling of shares – this led to prices tumbling.**

- This became known as the **Wall Street Crash**. On 24 October **(Black Thursday)**, 13 million shares were sold. On 29 October, 16 million were sold. The situation was made worse as banks, which also owned shares, sold in order to cover losses made when those who had borrowed money to buy shares were bankrupted.

191

193

Test yourself

1 What percentage of US families were below the minimum income needed for basic necessities?

2 When did the Wall Street Crash take place?

Check the facts

- The **Wall Street Crash** bankrupted many who had invested in shares. Others lost their savings when the smaller banks collapsed. Companies closed and workers became unemployed.

- As people lost their jobs, a vicious circle began, in which sales fell and even more people became unemployed. This led to the **Great Depression**.

> **By 1933 (the worst year), industrial production had fallen by 40 per cent and unemployment had reached 14 million.**

- Many farmers, unable to keep up mortgage payments, were evicted. The situation in the Mid-West was made worse by the **Dust Bowl** (a severe drought which caused harvests to fail).

919

- The Republican president, Herbert Hoover, believed in **laissez-faire** and **rugged individualism**. He therefore did little to deal with the problems.

- Without unemployment benefit, many relied on **soup kitchens** and charity hand-outs. The unemployed and homeless built **shanty towns** of cardboard shacks called **Hoovervilles**.

932

- Veteran soldiers tried to persuade Hoover to pay their war pensions early. In 1932, 20 000 (the **Bonus Army**) marched to Washington and built a Hooverville outside the White House. Hoover simply ordered the army to break it up.

- Eventually, Hoover began to take action. In 1930, he cut taxes. In 1931, he gave money to states to help build dams to provide work. In 1932, he agreed to an **Emergency Relief and Reconstruction Act**, which offered money to states that wished to help the unemployed. But it was too little, too late.

Test yourself

1 Who was president of the USA when the Great Depression began?

2 Name one of his two main beliefs.

3 Who were the 'Bonus Army'?

Check the facts

- The November 1932 presidential elections were won by a Democrat, **Franklin Delano Roosevelt**. Unlike his opponent (Hoover), Roosevelt believed the government should spend huge sums of money to end the economic crisis and help the American people.

- Although he had no specific policies, Roosevelt promised a **New Deal.** By the time he took over the presidency in March 1933, unemployment had reached 15 million and thousands of banks had collapsed.

- Roosevelt summonsed Congress to meet in an emergency session during his **First Hundred Days** to pass a series of laws to end the crisis. His first step was the **Emergency Banking Act**, which closed weaker banks and helped the stronger ones. It was designed to restore confidence in the banking system.

> **Roosevelt used the radio for fireside chats to explain his actions to the people.**

- Roosevelt then set up a series of government agencies – known as the **Alphabet Agencies** – to deal with the problems. These were designed to help the unemployed, revive the economy and create a fairer society.

- The main **New Deal** agencies were:

Federal Emergency Relief Agency (FERA)

Civil Works Administration (CWA)

Civilian Conservation Corps (CCC)

National Industrial Recovery Act (NIRA) – this included the Public Works Authority (PWA) and the 'Blue Eagle' scheme

Agricultural Adjustment Act (AAA)

Home Owners Loan Corporation (HOLC)

Farm Credit Association (FCA)

Tennessee Valley Authority (TVA)

1933

1945

Test yourself

1 When did Roosevelt take over as president after his election in November 1932?

2 What were his 'fireside chats'?

3 What were the 'Alphabet Agencies'?

The USA, 1919–45

Check the facts

- Although most ordinary people approved of Roosevelt's New Deal laws, his actions were opposed by:

Republicans, who did not agree with governments interfering with people's lives and the economy, or using tax payers' money to provide help for the poor and unemployed (they believed people should look after themselves).

Businessmen/industrialists, who objected to government interference, increased taxation to pay for relief programmes and Roosevelt's attempts to strengthen workers' rights.

States' Rights supporters, who believed that the federal (central) government was wrong to tell states how to help those suffering from the Depression.

The Supreme Court (the most serious), whose nine (mostly Republican) judges ruled that several New Deal laws were unconstitutional as they interfered with individual states. New Deal laws thrown out by the Supreme Court included the NIRA (1935) and the AAA (1936).

Radicals, such as Huey Long (who started a **Share Our Wealth** campaign) and Dr Frances Townsend (who also opposed the New Deal) – they believed Roosevelt was not doing enough for poor people.

- In 1935, Roosevelt began a second New Deal to extend the first and replace those laws thrown out by the Supreme Court, including the **National Labor Relations** (Wagner) **Act**, the **Social Security Act**, the **National Housing Act** and the **Works Progress Administration** (WPA). As a result, he won a massive victory in the 1936 presidential elections.

Test yourself

1 Give one reason why Republicans and businessmen opposed the New Deal.

2 How was the Supreme Court able to show its opposition to Roosevelt's New Deal?

3 Why did many radicals oppose the New Deal?

Roosevelt and the New Deal, 1933–45

BBC GCSE Check and Test: History

Roosevelt and the New Deal, 1933–45

Check the facts

- The **New Deal** managed to reduce unemployment from its peak in 1933, although problems remained. By 1937, consumer spending was still only 75 per cent of that for 1929.

- A second **depression** began in 1938 and caused unemployment to rise. By 1939, there were 9.5 million unemployed. This was due to:

  – a further decline in world trade

  – Roosevelt's decision in 1937 to reduce government spending (he believed the Depression was ending and wanted to avoid government debt).

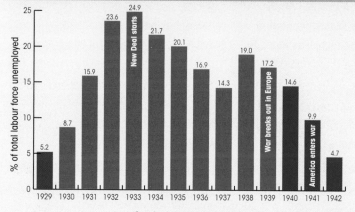

Graph showing unemployment in the USA during the 1930s

- The Republicans won control of Congress in the mid-term elections in 1938. This made it more difficult for Roosevelt to get new laws through to help the unemployed.

- Although the destruction of 'surplus' food and animals helped farmers, the higher prices made food too expensive for many poor people.

- The **Agricultural Adjustment Act** (AAA) quotas led to millions of poor black farmers being forced off the land.

- New Deal laws also allowed women and Black Americans to be paid less than white men – this affected millions of unskilled workers.

- It was the rearmament programme and entry into the Second World War that finally ended unemployment.

Test yourself

1 Give one reason why unemployment rose again in 1938.

2 What finally led unemployment to drop to near pre-Wall Street Crash levels?

www.bbc.co.uk/revision

1933

1945

Check the facts

- Despite **isolationism** (not becoming involved in the affairs of other countries), the Republicans maintained some involvement in Europe: the **Dawes Plan** (1924), the **Young Plan** (1929) and the **Kellogg–Briand Pact** (1928).

- However, isolationism did not apply to other areas of the world. Republican presidents of the 1920s and 1930s sent the US army into several states in Latin America (their **backyard**), while US plans to expand in Asia and the Pacific brought growing conflict with Japan.

> **Roosevelt at first continued with isolationism.**

- In 1934, the **Johnson Act** forbade loans to countries involved in wars, and two Neutrality Acts were passed in 1935 and 1937.

- However, the USA (with its own interests in China) objected when Japan invaded Manchuria in 1931 and mainland China in 1937.

- In November 1939, after the outbreak of war in Europe, Congress agreed to the **Cash and Carry Plan** and, in 1941, the **Lend-Lease Act**.

- Japanese plans for an economic empire in Asia led the USA to impose a trade boycott on Japan. In May 1941, the US imposed an oil and steel embargo and 'froze' Japanese assets in the US. Roosevelt also ordered the strengthening of US military bases in Hawaii and the Philippines.

933

> **As the US Pacific fleet was the main threat to Japanese ambitions, Japan attacked the US naval base at Pearl Harbor on 7 December.**

- The US declared war on Japan on 8 December and, on 11 December, on Germany and Italy.

945

Test yourself

1 In which two main areas did the USA intervene in the 1920s and 1930s?

2 Which country was the USA's main competitor for influence in Asia and the Pacific?

3 What were the Neutrality Acts?

Roosevelt and the New Deal, 1933–45

BBC GCSE Check and Test: History

Check the facts

- The Great Depression led many countries to adopt aggressive foreign policies to solve their economic difficulties. The first real example of this was Japan's invasion of Manchuria in 1931.

> **The League of Nations became increasingly ineffective, especially after 1933 when Hitler and the Nazis came to power in Germany.**

- One of Hitler's first acts in 1933 was to take Germany out of the **World Disarmament Conference**, which had begun in 1932. Later that same year, he took Germany out of the **League of Nations** and began secret rearmament.

- However, his attempt to achieve **Anschluss** (union) with Austria in 1934 was blocked by Italy, France and Britain, who later formed the Stresa Front. This loose alliance broke up in 1935, when Britain and France reluctantly opposed Italy's invasion of Abyssinia. It was further weakened when Britain signed a Naval Treaty with Nazi Germany later that same year.

- Hitler's main aims were: over-turning the Treaty of Versailles, uniting all German-speakers in a Greater Germany and taking Living Space in eastern Europe.

1930

> **All Hitler's aims would involve war.**

- Hitler's plans for war were strengthened in 1935, when the **Saarland** (an important industrial region administered by the League since 1919) voted to return to Germany. Hitler began to rearm openly, in defiance of the Treaty of Versailles.

1938

- His actions were encouraged by the League's failure to take effective action against Japanese and Italian aggression, and by the lack of unity between Britain and France.

Test yourself

1 In what year did Hitler take Germany out of the World Disarmament Conference and the League of Nations?

2 Give one reason why the Stresa Front broke up after 1935.

The Second World War, 1939–45

Check the facts

- After 1935, Hitler's actions became bolder. In March 1936, he ordered German troops to reoccupy the Rhineland, which, since 1919, had been a **demilitarised zone**. This was a clear violation of the Treaty of Versailles. Although Hitler's generals told him the German army was not ready for war, he gambled that Britain and France would do nothing.

> **In November 1936, the Stresa Front collapsed when Hitler persuaded Mussolini to sign the Rome–Berlin Axis with Nazi Germany.**

- The following year, these two fascist dictators decided to intervene in the Spanish Civil War (which had broken out in 1936) on the side of the right-wing Nationalists. Despite the League having formed a Non-Intervention Committee, Britain and France took no action and Hitler used it as an opportunity to test German military equipment.

- Also in 1937, Italy signed the **Anti-Comintern Pact**, which Germany and Japan had already formed – there was now a Rome–Berlin–Tokyo Axis.

- With friendship established between Italy and Germany, Hitler made a second attempt at Anschluss with Austria in March 1938. This time, it was successful. Again, despite it being against the Treaty of Versailles, Britain and France took no action. Hitler turned his attention to Czechoslovakia.

Central Europe after the Anschluss

Test yourself

1 What action did Hitler take in March 1936?

2 What was the Rome–Berlin Axis?

3 Why was Hitler able to achieve Anschluss with Austria in March 1938?

Causes of war, 1930–38

BBC GCSE Check and Test: History

Check the facts

- Britain and France followed a policy of **appeasement** in the 1930s. It was based on keeping Mussolini and Hitler happy by agreeing to most of their demands for land and 'revising' the Treaty of Versailles.

- Hitler noticed the League of Nations' weak actions over Japan's invasion of Manchuria in 1931 and Mussolini's invasion of Abyssinia in 1935.

> **In April 1938, the Czech Crisis began, when Hitler threatened the Sudetenland in Czechoslovakia.**

- This area of Czechoslovakia had belonged to the Habsburg empire and contained 3 million German-speakers. Hitler encouraged the local Nazis (led by Henlein) to stir up opposition to the Czech government. He then threatened to invade to 'protect' these German-speakers.

- France had set up the **Little Entente** with Czechoslovakia and the other **Successor** states in 1925, promising help if they were threatened by Germany. In 1938, **Daladier** (the new French prime minister) ignored this agreement – partly because **Chamberlain** (prime minister of Britain) made it clear that he would not support any French action.

- Instead, Chamberlain flew to Germany three times in September 1938, when Hitler increased his demands. Finally, Britain and France signed the **Munich Agreement**, accepting a German takeover of the Sudetenland. This gave Hitler the Czech border defences and armaments works. The Czechs were not invited to the Munich Conference.

- Historians are divided over whether appeasement made the Second World War more likely (by encouraging Hitler) or whether Chamberlain acted wisely, in view of Britain's inability to fight a war in 1938 and thus the need for time to rearm.

1938

Test yourself

1 Who were Daladier and Chamberlain?

2 Why was the Sudetenland important?

Final steps, 1938–9

Check the facts

> After Munich, Hitler threatened the rest of Czechoslovakia and, in March 1939, German troops invaded.

- Once again, Britain and France took no action. Hitler concluded that provided he accepted Germany's western borders, he was free to expand eastwards.

- Hitler's next target was Poland. However, at the end of March 1939, Britain and France promised to defend Polish independence. Hitler did not take this seriously, even when Britain introduced **conscription** for all males aged 20–21.

- Hitler then worked to get an agreement with the USSR to prevent it opposing his plans to invade Poland.

> Hitler believed that without Soviet help, Britain and France would not help Poland.

- Stalin had tried for some time to get an agreement with Britain and France. He had promised to help Czechoslovakia, if Britain and France took action over the Sudetenland. But Stalin had not been invited to the Munich Conference and became suspicious when Britain delayed further discussions in the summer of 1939. He wondered if Britain and France were secretly encouraging Hitler to attack the USSR.

- In August 1939, to gain time to build up Soviet defences, Stalin agreed to a ten-year Non-Aggression Pact with Nazi Germany. This included a secret clause to divide Poland between them and to allow the Soviet Union to take over the Baltic States. This extra territory was to provide the USSR with a **buffer zone** against the expected German invasion.

Test yourself

1 What action did Hitler order in March 1939?

2 Why did Stalin sign the Nazi-Soviet Non-Aggresssion Pact in August 1939?

Final steps, 1938-9

939

BBC GCSE Check and Test: History

Check the facts

Theatres of War, 1939–45

> On 1 September 1939, German troops invaded Poland. Two days later, Britain and France declared war on Germany – the Second World War had begun.

- Using **Blitzkrieg** ('lightning war') tactics, German armies achieved rapid success. This new method of warfare was based on the use of planes, tanks, paratroops and motorised infantry – its surprise, speed and overwhelming force quickly knocked out an enemy. Poland was defeated in less than a month.

- However, Britain and France did not send help. Until April 1940, they were not really involved in the war.

> This period is sometimes known as the Phoney War, even though German U-boats and mines sunk several Allied ships.

- Instead, Hitler concentrated on conquering the countries on Germany's northern and western borders. In April 1940, Denmark was occupied and Norway invaded – a small British force failed to stop Germany securing control of the region. In May, Norway surrendered and Hitler ordered invasions of the Low Countries and France.

- By the end of May 1940, the Netherlands, Belgium and Luxembourg had been defeated, and the British Expeditionary Force (sent to help France) had to be evacuated from Dunkirk in **Operation Dynamo**.

- This encouraged Mussolini to declare war on Britain and France and, on 22 June 1940, France surrendered. The Germans occupied northern France, while Marshal Pétain was allowed to run the south (called **Vichy France**, as his headquarters were in Vichy), provided he cooperated with the Germans. Britain was now on its own, and remained without allies until June 1941.

1939

1945

Test yourself

1 What is meant by the term 'Blitzkrieg'?

2 When did France surrender to the Germans?

Check the facts

On 22 June 1941, Hitler launched his long-term plan (Operation Barbarossa) to invade the USSR.

- Operation Barbarossa was originally planned for the early spring (to defeat the Soviet Union before winter). It was delayed (a) because Hitler had been forced to divert troops to help the Italians in North Africa and the Balkans and (b) because of bad weather.

- The USSR was taken by surprise, as Stalin believed that Hitler would not attack until Britain had been defeated. As a result, the Germans – with an army over 5 million strong – destroyed most of the Soviet airforce on the ground and advanced deep into the Soviet Union. Over 700 000 Red Army troops were captured.

- By October 1941, the USSR seemed on the verge of collapse. However, as the Russians retreated, they moved factories and workers behind the Ural Mountains. What they were unable to remove was destroyed **(Scorched Earth Policy)**.

The Russian winter began early. The German army, not equipped for a winter campaign, ground to a halt. The Red Army then launched a counter-attack in December 1941.

- Hitler ordered new offensives and devoted over 75 per cent of his forces to the Eastern Front. In June 1942, he split his southern army in two, as he was determined to capture Stalingrad.

- From November 1942 to January 1943, the Russians fought back. Finally, what remained of the German Sixth Army was forced to surrender. This was an important **turning point** in the war.

- In July 1943, the Russians won the Battle of Kursk and, from September 1943, the Germans were in retreat. Over 90 per cent of Germany's total military casualties were on the Eastern Front.

1939

1945

Test yourself

1 When did 'Operation Barbarossa' begin?

2 Which battle was the turning point in the war on the Eastern Front (and of the Second World War as a whole)?

Theatres of War, 1939–45

BBC GCSE Check and Test: History

Check the facts

- Although the USA did not enter the Second World War until December 1941, Roosevelt had already begun to abandon the traditional US policies of isolationism and neutrality.

- At first, the USA got involved via the **Lend-Lease Scheme** of March 1941. This loaned US military equipment to Britain, which had to be carried in British ships. After 1941, US ships also transported supplies to Britain.

- It was important for Nazi Germany to prevent these supplies reaching Britain from the USA.

> **This naval contest became known as the Battle of the Atlantic.**

- At first, German U-boats succeeded in destroying large numbers of merchant ships. They did this despite Allied tactics involving the use of a convoy system, with destroyers providing protection for the merchant ships.

- These heavy losses led to severe shortages of food and raw materials in Britain. By March 1943, it seemed Britain was losing the ability to continue with the war.

> **However, an important turning point took place in April 1943, when German radio codes were broken by the Allies.**

- From May 1943, the Allies began to destroy around fifty German submarines a month. This success was also the result of improved tactics and technology:
  - faster escort ships
  - radar and asdic to find submarines
  - long-range aircraft.

- In March 1944, the Germans ended their attacks on convoys – the battle of the Atlantic had been won by the Allies.

1939

1945

Test yourself

1 What was the Lend-Lease Scheme of March 1941?

2 What was the 'Battle of the Atlantic' about?

3 Why was April 1943 an important turning point in the Battle of the Atlantic?

Check the facts

- In August 1940, an Italian army occupied British Somaliland. In September, it invaded Egypt to capture the Suez Canal (a vital British shipping route). In October, Italy invaded Greece.

- The Italians did badly in Greece and had to divert troops from Africa. In December 1940, a British counter-attack in Egypt resulted in the capture of the Italian colony of Libya.

- In the Balkans, Yugoslavia refused to ally with Hitler. So, in April 1941, Germany invaded Yugoslavia. It also invaded Greece, in order to help the Italians. By the end of May, both countries had been defeated.

> **In April 1941, Hitler sent the Afrika Korps, commanded by Rommel, to Africa to help the Italians.**

- Soon, Libya had been retaken and Rommel invaded **Egypt**.

- In November 1941, with most of Germany's military resources on the Eastern Front, the British launched **Operation Crusader**. However, in May 1942, Rommel defeated the British Eighth Army at Tobruk.

- In August 1942, Montgomery took charge of the Eighth Army. In October/November, he defeated Rommel at the Battle of El Alamein. This proved a **turning point**, and the Allies launched Operation Torch against the Afrika Korps. Rommel surrendered in Tunisia and, by May 1943, the Allies controlled North Africa. At the same time, Axis forces were retreating from the Balkans.

- This allowed an Anglo-American invasion of Sicily in July. In September, the invasion of mainland Italy began. **Mussolini** was overthrown and Italy sided with the Allies – but Hitler sent German forces to slow the Allies.

Test yourself

1 Why was Egypt important to Britain?

2 At which battle did Montgomery defeat Rommel's Afrika Korps?

3 Why was this battle an important turning point in the Second World War?

Theatres of War, 1939–45

BBC GCSE Check and Test: History

Theatres of War, 1939–45

Check the facts

- Since 1931, Japan (with the third largest army in the world) had been expanding in Asia. The USA, which had long had its own interests in the region, objected to Japan's invasion of China in 1937.

- The invasion of China was expensive, so Japan decided to take over parts of South-East Asia to form a **Greater East Asia Co-Prosperity Sphere**. This would provide Japan with oil and other raw materials.

- When Japan invaded French Indo-China in July 1941, the USA banned the sale of oil, aircraft and iron to Japan, and froze all Japanese assets in the USA until Japan made peace with China.

- Oil and iron existed in the British and Dutch colonies in the region, but Japan's navy was not stong enough to face an Anglo-American force.

> **In December 1941, Japan launched a surprise attack on the main base of the US Pacific Fleet at Pearl Harbor.**

- This attack brought the Asian-Pacific War into the Second World War. At first, Japanese forces were victorious in South-East Asia and, by August 1942, had conquered most of the region. Thousands of British and US troops had also been captured.

- However, in May 1942, Japan had suffered its first defeat at the **Battle of Midway**. This ended Japanese naval supremacy and allowed US forces to advance. In June 1943, the USA began submarine warfare against Japanese shipping.

- From January 1944, Allied forces used the tactic of **island hopping**, i.e. ignoring the smaller islands occupied by Japan in order to concentrate their forces on the more strategic islands.

1939

1945

Test yourself

1 Name one action the USA took when Japan attacked French Indo-China in July 1941.

2 What was the purpose of the 'Greater East Asia Co-Prosperity Sphere'?

3 What do you understand by the term 'island hopping'?

Check the facts

- 1943 saw the Allies on the offensive. The **area bombing** of Germany (to destroy railways, docks, factories, etc.) that had begun in 1942 was stepped up.

- These intensive bombing campaigns also targeted civilian areas.

> **In July 1943, over 50 000 were killed by the firestorms in Hamburg.**

- Since 1942, Stalin had pressed for an Allied **second front** in western Europe to relieve pressure on the USSR. Finally, on 6 June 1944 **(D-Day)** 'Operation Overlord' began. Over a million Allied troops, commanded by Eisenhower, landed in Normandy in ten days. The Soviet Union launched a major offensive in eastern Europe to coincide with this and, in August, also advanced in the south.

- In December 1944, the Allied advance in western Europe slowed down. The last major German counter-offensive was defeated in the **Battle of the Bulge** in January 1945.

> **In May 1945, Germany surrendered.**

- Since March 1945, the USA had begun a massive bombing campaign against Japan from captured island airfields. Over 80 000 civilians were killed in just one raid on Tokyo. Millions fled from the cities as firebomb attacks destroyed 25 per cent of civilian homes. This deprived Japan's armaments industries of vital production workers.

- At the end of July 1945, Japan rejected an offer of an armistice and the USSR officially joined the war against Japan.

- Then, in August 1945, the USA decided to drop its new secret weapon **(atomic bombs)** on **Hiroshima** and **Nagasaki**. At the same time, the Soviet Union invaded Manchuria. Japan then surrendered, so ending the Second World War.

Test yourself

1 Why did Stalin call repeatedly for a 'second front' in Europe?

2 What was 'Operation Overlord'?

3 Why was the USA able to mount a massive bombing campaign against Japan during 1945?

Theatres of War, 1939–45

BBC GCSE Check and Test: History

Check the facts

- By the end of the Second World War, the USA and the USSR were the two dominant superpowers – although the USA had avoided the destruction suffered by the USSR. European countries, such as Britain, France and Germany, which had been powerful before the war, were economically weakened or in ruins.

- Although the USA and the USSR were Allies, there were tensions between them, some of which went back to 1917 and the Bolshevik Revolution.

> **The USA and the USSR believed in two different economic and political systems – capitalism and communism. This has been called the 'Great Contest'.**

- Capitalists believe in private ownership of the economy and, usually, political democracy. Communists believe in state ownership and, under Stalin, operated one-party rule.

- The Soviet Union, since 1914, had been invaded three times through eastern European countries ruled by hostile right-wing governments. During the Civil War, Britain and the USA had supported the Whites.

- After 1933, Stalin thought that Britain and France, by appeasement, were encouraging Hitler to attack the USSR. He also became suspicious over the delay in opening up a second front against Nazi Germany in western Europe.

- At the end of the war, with its economy in ruins and over 20 million dead, Stalin feared the USA might use its nuclear weapons' monopoly to destroy the USSR, which was then the only communist state in the world.

- The USA and the West feared that Stalin would try to spread communism across war-devastated Europe and so destroy capitalism and opportunities for investments and profits.

194
1945

Test yourself

1 What do you understand by the term 'superpower'?

2 What was the 'Great Contest'?

3 Give one reason why Stalin was suspicious of the West before 1945.

Check the facts

- During the Second World War, differences between the USA and the USSR had been put to one side in order to defeat Nazi Germany. However, disagreements over the opening of a **second front** emerged in the Grand Alliance after 1942.

- Stalin was desperate for the opening of a second front to relieve pressure on the Soviet Union. By 1944, there were 228 Axis divisions on the Eastern Front, compared to 61 in western Europe. This meant most of Hitler's armies were fighting against the USSR, causing massive destruction and putting the USSR under severe pressure.

- In November 1943, the Big Three met at the **Tehran Conference**. Despite the continued delay in opening a second front, outline agreements were reached on redrawing the Polish borders and preventing any anti-Soviet alliance in eastern Europe after the war.

- In October 1944, Churchill went to Moscow. His visit resulted in the **percentages agreement**, which decided on spheres of influence in eastern Europe after the war. Roosevelt, though not present, was informed and made no objections.

- At the Yalta Conference in February 1945, initial agreements over Poland and Germany (including reparations) were reached. Stalin also agreed to join the war against Japan once Germany had been defeated. Then, in April, Roosevelt died.

> **Roosevelt was replaced by Vice-President Truman, who took a more anti-communist line.**

- Germany had been defeated by the time of the next Conference at Potsdam in July-August 1945. This time, serious differences emerged over German reparations, the government of Poland and the presence of the Red Army in eastern Europe. However, there was agreement that the USSR could receive eastern Poland, while Poland would be compensated with German territory.

Test yourself

1 Which two Allied leaders made the 'percentages agreement' in October 1944?

2 How did Roosevelt's death in April 1945 increase tensions between the USA and the USSR?

Origins of the Cold War, 1941–5

BBC GCSE Check and Test: History

Origins of the Cold War, 1941–5

Check the facts

- During the **Potsdam Conference**, Truman decided to drop **atomic bombs** on Japan without informing Stalin. He also decided not to share the technology of this secret weapon with the USSR. Although Stalin ordered Soviet scientists to build a Soviet bomb, the USA had a nuclear monopoly for the next four years.

- Stalin feared the USA would use its superiority to blackmail the war-devastated Soviet Union. One response was to step up Soviet control of eastern Europe. This took place between 1945 and 1948. He said these countries were to become **buffer zones**, giving the USSR greater protection from any future invasion.

- The West, however, saw these moves as the first part of Stalin's plans to take over the whole of Europe.

> **Within a year of the Second World War ending, growing tensions between the Allies resulted in the start of what became known as the Cold War.**

- Differences over Germany widened. The USSR wanted substantial reparations and was reluctant to allow Germany to re-industrialise, while the USA now opposed massive reparations, wanting to rebuild the German economy as quickly as possible instead.

- As relations deteriorated, Churchill made a speech in March 1946 about growing Soviet control in eastern Europe creating an **Iron Curtain** between East and West.

- The Cold War soon led to an arms race, control of neighbouring countries, spying, propaganda and substitute 'hot' wars, in which each superpower helped its allies fight the other superpower or its allies in regional wars.

194
194!

Test yourself

1 How did the dropping of atomic bombs on Japan contribute to a breakdown in relations between the USA and the USSR?

2 How did Stalin explain the Soviet takeover of eastern Europe?

3 What did Churchill mean by the phrase 'Iron Curtain'?

Check the facts

- In February 1946, a US diplomat called Kennan sent a report to the US government about the USSR. This **Long Telegram** stated that the Soviet Union was determined to expand.

- This started the new US policy of **containment** of communism. Those who believed (like Roosevelt had) that Stalin was prepared to make concessions in return for security were forced to resign from Truman's administration.

- By 1947, most West European countries were in a serious economic crisis, and Communist Parties in Italy and France were winning votes in elections. Then, in February 1947, Britain said it could no longer afford to support the Greek Royalists in their **civil war** against the Greek Communists.

- The USA believed in the **'Rotten Apple'** theory (similar to the 'Domino Theory'). It feared that if Greece went communist, other countries in the region would follow.

> **In March 1947, Truman announced the Truman Doctrine.**

- The Truman Doctrine said the USA would give military help to all countries resisting 'armed minorities' or 'outside pressure'. As part of this, Truman set up the National Security Council (NSC) and the Central Intelligence Agency (CIA).

- Truman decided to give massive economic aid to western Europe and rebuild Germany.

> **The Marshall Plan – or Marshall Aid, as it was sometimes known – was announced in June 1947.**

- Although aid was available for all countries, both sides saw it as a way of weakening Soviet control of eastern Europe. By 1952, when the aid ended, the gap in living standards between East and West Europe had widened. Marshall Aid had also helped the US economy.

Test yourself

1 What was the 'Long Telegram'?

2 Explain the meaning of the term 'containment'.

3 Give one aim of the Marshall Plan.

BBC GCSE Check and Test: History

Check the facts

- As Cold War tensions developed after 1945, Stalin decided to increase Soviet control of eastern Europe. He felt particularly vulnerable as the Soviet Union had suffered great destruction during the war, whereas the USA was the world's richest power.

> Stalin also feared the USA's desire to revive Germany, which, since 1900, had twice invaded the USSR.

- Using a variety of methods, including **rigging elections**, Stalin ensured that communists came to power in eastern European countries and accepted Soviet control.

- In 1946, Bulgaria was the first country to have a communist-dominated government; in 1947, Hungary, Poland and Romania followed suit. The last to come under communist control was Czechoslovakia, in 1948.

- By then, a serious crisis had broken out over Germany. Although Germany had been temporarily split into four administrative zones, it had been agreed at Potsdam to treat it as one economic unit. However, the question of reparations caused growing conflict between the USSR (who wanted massive compensation) and the other Allies (who were against this).

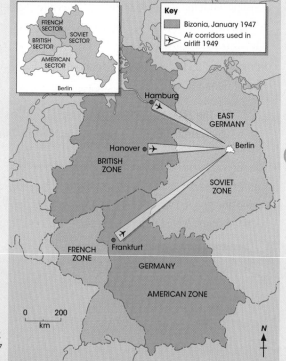

Key

- Bizonia, January 1947
- Air corridors used in airlift 1949

Divided Germany, 1945–7

Check the facts

- In January 1947, the USA and Britain merged their zones to form **Bizonia**. Stalin feared this was the first step to reviving the economy of a new West German state. As Bizonia contained 75 per cent of Germany's population and most of its industry, he saw this as a future military threat. These fears increased when France added its zone, to make **Trizonia**.

- Then, in June 1947 – without consulting the USSR – the West introduced a new currency **(the Deutschmark)** into its zones, including West Berlin, which was inside the Soviet zone.

- Stalin was opposed to the idea of a separate West German state and replied by cutting off all transport links to West Berlin. This became known as the **Berlin Blockade.**

> The **Berlin Crisis** **was the first serious Cold War conflict between the two sides.**

- The West responded with the massive **Berlin Airlift**, in which tons of food, fuel and other vital supplies were flown into West Berlin. In May 1949, Stalin called off the Blockade.

- The Berlin Crisis speeded up Western moves to set up a separate West German state. In May 1949, the new **Federal Republic of Germany** (FRG) was set up. In October, the USSR transformed its zone into the new **German Democratic Republic** (GDR). This division of Germany soon came to symbolise the Cold War division of Europe into two mutually suspicious and hostile camps.

Test yourself

1 Why did the USSR insist on massive reparations from Germany after the Second World War?

2 What was 'Trizonia'?

3 How did the West respond to the Berlin Blockade ?

Check the facts

- In February 1948, during the Berlin Crisis of 1947–9, the countries of western Europe formed the **Brussels Treaty Organisation**.

> **In January 1949, the USA joined the Brussels Treaty Organisation and it became the North Atlantic Treaty Organisation (NATO).**

- The USA said **NATO** was a defensive alliance against the Soviet 'threat'. The USSR was alarmed, as it had no similar alliance until 1955 when the Warsaw Pact was formed. It was particularly concerned as NATO had the USA's nuclear monopoly, with its ability to launch atomic weapons against the USSR. Even after 1955, NATO continued to have overall superiority.

- At this time, the USSR was only a regional power compared to the USA, which was already a global power. The USSR had no allies outside Europe; its allies were the poor and weak East European states.

> **The formation of NATO intensified the arms race (conventional and nuclear) between the USSR and the USA.**

- In 1945, the USSR's Red Army had numbered 11 million, while the USA had 12 million troops. After the war, both armies were reduced. It wasn't long before the Red Army had dropped to 3 million, although it remained the largest army in Europe. While the USA also greatly reduced its army, its forces remained technically superior.

- More important was the question of **nuclear weapons** – the USSR did not test its first **atomic bomb** (A-bomb) until August 1949. By then, the USA was already working on a powerful nuclear weapon – the **hydrogen bomb** (H-bomb).

194

Test yourself

1 When was NATO formed?

2 What was the Soviet Union's 1955 alliance called?

3 When was the USA's nuclear weapons monopoly ended?

Check the facts

> In October 1949, the Chinese Communists came to power in China. This led to McCarthyism in the USA and increased Cold War tensions.

- In April 1950, the NSC 68 document advised Truman to 'roll back' communism. Tensions rose in Korea, which after the war had been divided (along the 38th parallel) into a **communist North** and a **capitalist South**. Both sides were preparing to invade the other to reunify their country.

> In June 1950, North Korea invaded the South and quickly conquered most of it.

- The USA (believing in the **Domino Theory**) decided to use the UN to 'contain' this communist threat. The USSR (boycotting the UN in protest at the USA's refusal to allow Communist China a seat) was unable to veto this.

- Most of the UN troops were Americans, and the US/UN force was commanded by **US General MacArthur**. By October, North Korean troops had been pushed back over the border.

- Then, in breach of the UN resolution, Truman ordered MacArthur to invade the North. When US troops reached the border with China, the Chinese government sent in an army to help the North. By January 1951, US/UN forces had been pushed back across the 38th parallel.

- A **stalemate** developed. In July 1951, talks for a truce began. Meanwhile, the USA developed the H-bomb in 1952. In January 1953, **Eisenhower** became US President. In March, Stalin died. In July, an armistice was finally signed.

> Later that month, the USSR exploded its first H-bomb.

Test yourself

1 Why did Cold War tensions in Asia increase in 1949?

2 How was the USA able to get the UN to agree to send troops against North Korea?

3 When did the fighting in the Korean War end?

Hotspots since 1945

BBC GCSE Check and Test: History

Check the facts

- Stalin died in 1953. The new Soviet leadership wanted to reduce Cold War tensions, and a **thaw** soon began. In 1955, **Khrushchev** became overall leader of the USSR. He believed the Cold War's arms race was too expensive. His policy of **peaceful coexistence** aimed to concentrate on economic competition with the West.

- Khrushchev tried to reduce tensions by agreeing to end the division of Austria in return for it not joining NATO. But the arms race continued.

> **In 1955, Khrushchev formed the Warsaw Pact to counter NATO, which had been set up in 1949.**

- In 1956, at the Twentieth Congress of the Soviet Communist Party, Khrushchev attacked Stalin's actions. **De-Stalinisation** in the USSR, and the ending of Cominform, encouraged eastern Europeans to think they could reduce Soviet domination. Some reforms were allowed in Poland.

- In Hungary, huge demonstrations forced Rakosi, a **hardliner**, to resign. He was replaced by Nagy. When Nagy tried to take Hungary out of the Warsaw Pact, Soviet forces invaded.

> **In November 1956, the Hungarian Revolt was crushed.**

- Nagy was deposed and later executed. The West did not intervene, because of the Suez Crisis following the British and French (and Israeli) attack on Egypt.

- A new crisis over Germany and Berlin broke out in 1958. Relations improved at the **Camp David** summit in 1959, but deteriorated in 1960 because of the U2 (US spyplane) Incident. Thousands of East Germans fled to the West. In 1961, East Germany built the **Berlin Wall** between East and West Berlin.

194

Test yourself

1 When did Khrushchev form the Warsaw Pact?

2 Why did Soviet troops invade Hungary in November 1956?

Hotspots since 1945

Check the facts

- Since 1959, after a revolution against Batista (a corrupt and brutal dictator supported by the USA), Cuba has been ruled by **Castro.**

- However, since the 1820s, the USA had seen Latin America and the Caribbean as its **backyard**. In 1948, the USA had set up the Organisation of American States (OAS) to prevent the spread of communism.

- The USA, the main purchaser of Cuba's sugar and tobacco, became concerned when Castro began land reform and said Cuba would be neutral in the Cold War. Disagreements over economic policies led Eisenhower to stop buying Cuban sugar. Castro then sold the sugar to the USSR.

- In 1961, the USA broke off diplomatic relations with Cuba and helped Cuban exiles in an unsuccessful attempt to invade Cuba. This **Bay of Pigs** incident led Castro to ask for Soviet protection.

- Khrushchev, worried by the US nuclear superiority and especially US missiles in Italy and Turkey, decided to put Soviet missiles on Cuba (only 90 miles away from the USA).

- US spy-planes noticed missile sites (without missiles) in September 1962.

> **Kennedy imposed a naval blockade to block Soviet ships carrying the missiles.**

- A Third World War seemed near, but the **Cuban Missile Crisis** ended when Khruschchev agreed to withdraw the missiles – in return, the USA secretly promised not to invade Cuba and to remove its missiles from Turkey.

- In 1963, a 'hot line' between the White House and the Kremlin was set up. A **Nuclear Test Ban Treaty** was also signed.

Hotspots since 1945

Test yourself

1 What area did the USA see as its 'backyard'?

2 Why did Castro ask for Soviet protection in 1961?

3 How was the Cuban Missile Crisis brought to an end?

B B C GCSE Check and Test: History

Check the facts

- Vietnam was another Cold War **hotspot.** It was part of French Indo-China, where, before 1945, the **Vietminh** (a nationalist army led by the communist Ho Chi Minh) had been fighting for independence from the French. Because of the **Cold War**, the USA had been supporting the French.

- In 1954, the French were defeated at Dien Bien Phu and withdrew. At the Geneva Conference, Vietnam was temporarily divided along the **seventeenth parallel** into the **North** and the **South**, with elections to take place in 1956.

> North Vietnam **was ruled by the** Communists, **while** South Vietnam **was ruled by a wealthy** landlord class.

- Diem, who became the leader of the South in 1955, refused to hold the elections. In 1960, communists in the South then formed the **Viet Cong** to fight Diem. The USA sent military 'advisers' and weapons to the South, while the Viet Cong were helped by North Vietnam. North Vietnam, which received military equipment from the USSR, sent supplies to the Viet Cong along the Ho Chi Minh Trail.

- By 1962, Kennedy had greatly increased US aid, but Diem continued to lose ground to the Viet Cong. In November 1963, the CIA encouraged generals in the South to overthrow Diem.

Map of Vietnam

194

- When Kennedy was assassinated that same month, Vice-President Johnson took over – he was committed to increasing US involvement. After the Gulf of Tonkin Incident, the US Congress passed the **Tonkin Resolution**, allowing Johnson to take 'all necessary steps' to defend South Vietnam. In 1965, he escalated the war by launching **Operation Rolling Thunder** – a massive bombing campaign against North Vietnam. By 1969, there were over 500 000 US troops in South Vietnam.

- However, in 1968, the Viet Cong and North Vietnamese troops had launched the **Tet Offensive**, which, although defeated, showed how unsuccessful US intervention had been. By then, many in the US had become opposed to the war and Johnson decided not to stand in the 1968 elections.

> **There was particular concern over the use of napalm, defoliants and 'search and destroy' missions, one of which resulted in the My Lai Massacre.**

- The new president, Richard Nixon, decided to end US involvement and began a policy of 'Vietnamisation', although US bombing raids were stepped up. Soon, with Cold War relations improving in what was called **détente**, peace negotiations began.

> **In 1973, the US withdrew its forces from Vietnam. In 1975, Vietnam was finally reunited, after the North invaded the South.**

Test yourself

1 What, according to the Geneva Agreement, should have taken place in Vietnam in 1956?

2 Who were the Viet Cong?

3 What was 'Operation Rolling Thunder'?

4 When did the USA withdraw its troops from South Vietnam?

Check the facts

- By the late 1960s, both superpowers wanted to reduce Cold War tensions and halt the arms race, because:

  - the Cuban Missile Crisis, and various weapons systems errors, had brought nuclear war near
  - there was increased opposition to nuclear weapons
  - other countries were developing nuclear weapons.

- The Soviet economy (less wealthy than the USA's) was struggling under the huge cost of matching the US lead in nuclear weapons. The USSR was also worried at signs of growing cooperation between the USA and China.

- The USA was keen to use China to put pressure on the USSR to make concessions, while China wanted to increase trade with the West and saw the USA as an ally against the USSR. The USA was also keen to pull out of Vietnam and reconsider its Cold War strategy.

- This led to **détente** (a lessening of tensions and a greater willingness to negotiate). The main leaders who developed and pursued this policy were presidents Nixon and Carter in the USA, Brezhnev in the USSR and Mao Zedong in China.

- Various agreements resulted in the late 1960s and the 1970s. In 1968, there was the Nuclear Non-Proliferation Treaty. In 1971, the USA finally allowed Communist China to join the UN. In 1972, Nixon visited China.

- Also in 1972, the USA and the USSR agreed the SALT 1 Treaty. In 1975, both sides signed the **Helsinki Agreement**, which confirmed Europe's 1945 borders and dealt with human rights.

- However, the arms race continued; there were verification problems with SALT 1, and the USSR often ignored the human rights agreed at Helsinki. Despite this, a draft SALT 2 Treaty was agreed in 1978.

194

Test yourself

1 What do you understand by the term 'détente'?

2 Name one US president associated with the policy of détente.

Check the facts

- Despite détente, Soviet leaders maintained control over eastern Europe, as events in Czechoslovakia (1968) and Poland (1980) showed.
- In 1946, the Czech Communist Party had won 38 per cent of the vote in free elections. After 1948, Czechoslovakia had been tightly ruled. By the mid-1960s, its economy was stagnating.
- In 1966, **Czech students** demonstrated for greater political freedom and less Soviet control.
- In 1968, reform Communists forced Novotny, a hardline Stalinist, to resign. He was replaced by **Dubcek**.
- Dubcek announced his Action Plan to create **'Socialism with a human face'**. Controls on the mass media were lifted and people were allowed to criticise the government.

> **This was known as the Prague Spring.**

- The Prague Spring led the USSR and other eastern European countries to send the **Warsaw Letter**, expressing their fears. Dubcek made it clear he would not take Czechoslovakia out of the Warsaw Pact, but insisted on reform.
- But, in August 1968, Warsaw Pact forces invaded – Dubcek was dismissed. In November, the **Brezhnev Doctrine** said no Warsaw Pact member could leave and multi-party systems were prohibited.
- In Poland, economic problems in the 1970s led to strikes. In 1980, the government raised food prices.

> **Many Polish strikers formed Solidarity, an independent trade union – one of its main leaders was Lech Walesa.**

- Solidarity began to make political demands that went against the Brezhnev Doctrine.
- This worried the USSR, which, in 1981, put pressure on the Polish Communists to take action. Martial law was imposed, Solidarity was banned and Walesa was arrested.

Test yourself

1 Which Czechoslovak Communist leader tried to create 'Socialism with a human face'?
2 What was the Brezhnev Doctrine?
3 When was the Polish Solidarity trade union banned?

Hotspots since 1945

BBC GCSE Check and Test: History

Hotspots since 1945

Check the facts

- By 1979, **détente** was under increasing strain. This was partly because a series of revolutions in western Europe (Portugal and Spain) and the developing world (Iran and Nicaragua) had deprived the USA of several allies.

- Although the USSR had not been involved in these revolutions, US politicians blamed the Soviet Union for them. The USA also attacked the USSR for not implementing the Helsinki Agreement on human rights.

- Then, in 1979, the USSR sent troops into Afghanistan to help the new communist government deal with Islamic fundamentalists. This was strongly condemned by US President Carter – it surprised the USSR, as Afghanistan had unofficially been seen as in the Soviet sphere. In 1980, when Reagan took over from Carter, détente ended as a second Cold War began.

> **Reagan was anti-communist and claimed the USA had fallen behind the USSR in the nuclear arms race.**

- Reagan doubled military expenditure and pushed ahead with new weapons, such as the neutron bomb, Cruise, Pershing 2 and MX. He also began the **Strategic Defence Initiative** (SDI, or **Star Wars**). Disarmament talks (START) between the two superpowers broke down in 1985.

> **In 1985, Gorbachev became leader of the USSR. He wanted to improve living standards and industrial efficiency and increase political freedom in the Soviet Union.**

- Gorbachev believed attempting to keep up with US weapons developments was ruining the Soviet economy (because the USSR was less wealthy than the USA, it had to devote 25 per cent of government spending to match the USA's 7 per cent). As a result, he was determined not to follow the USA in Reagan's latest escalation of the arms race.

194

Test yourself

1 In which country did Soviet troops intervene in December 1979?

2 Who replaced Carter as US president in 1980?

3 What reason did this president give for beginning a new arms race?

Check the facts

- Gorbachev wanted to end this new arms race and decided to end the Cold War. Meetings took place between him and Reagan at Reykjavik in 1986 and in Washington in 1987.

> **Gorbachev made such important concessions on nuclear weapons – basically accepting US superiority – that Reagan was forced to agree.**

- The major agreements were:
  - the Intermediate Nuclear Forces (INF) Treaty, 1987, to reduce medium-range missiles
  - the Strategic Arms Reductions Talks (START) Treaty, 1991, to reduce long-range missiles (made with Bush, who replaced Reagan in 1988).

- Gorbachev and Reagan also agreed to reduce NATO and the Warsaw Pact's conventional forces.

- Gorbachev ended Soviet intervention in Afghanistan and announced that the USSR would no longer intervene in eastern Europe to stop democratic reforms. This ended the Brezhnev Doctrine of 1968.

- Gorbachev urged East European governments to adopt the reforms he was making in the USSR (**perestroika, glasnost** and **demokratizatsiya**). From 1988 onwards, reforms took place and Soviet control ended.

- In 1989, Solidarity was legalised and won a majority in the Polish elections.

> **In 1989, the Berlin Wall was knocked down, and Germany was reunited in 1990.**

- In July 1991, the Warsaw Pact was dissolved – although NATO continued.

- Gorbachev's policies were opposed by old-style communists in the USSR. Economic problems and nationalist unrest increased their unease and, in August 1991, they tried to overthrow Gorbachev.

- Although the coup failed, the USSR ended in December, after Russia formed the CIS with two other Soviet republics. The 'Great Contest' and the Cold War were over – the USA was the only remaining superpower.

Test yourself

1 What was agreed by (i) the INF Treaty in 1987 (ii) the START Treaty in 1991?

2 When was Germany reunited?

3 When did the Soviet Union come to an end?

Superpower relations since 1945

Hotspots since 1945

BBC GCSE Check and Test: History

Britain before the First World War, 1900–14

Check the facts

- When Queen Victoria died in 1901, Britain had an empire covering 20 per cent of the world's land surface – this provided raw materials and markets for British industry.

- Since 1875, Britain had been involved in the **Scramble for Africa**. This had brought Britain into conflict with France and the new state of Germany, formed in 1871.

- With high industrial production and exports, and the largest empire in the world, Britain seemed the most powerful country in the world.

190

191

> **The period 1901–14 became known as Britain's Golden Age.**

- However, many of Britain's 'old' or 'staple' industries (e.g. coal, iron and textiles) faced increased competition from Germany, Japan and the USA. These countries put more money into modernising their factories and were quick to develop new industries, such as chemicals and electrical goods.

- Despite Britain's great wealth, there was much poverty – especially in the industrial towns. This had been shown by the Boer War of 1899–1902, when many volunteers were declared unfit for military service.

- Generally, real wages for most workers had improved since the 1880s, largely due to the increase in trade unionism amongst unskilled and semi-skilled workers. However, many employers wanted Parliament and the courts to limit successful strikes.

- The Taff Vale Case in 1901 was a setback for unions and came when prices were rising at a faster rate than wages. This led the unions to turn to Parliament.

- At first, many union members supported the Liberals. However, in 1900, the TUC set up the Labour Representation Committee (LRC). This put pressure on the Liberals.

Test yourself

1 Why were colonies seen as being important for industrial nations?

2 When did the TUC set up the Labour Representation Committee?

www.bbc.co.uk/revision

Check the facts

- The Conservatives had dominated British politics since 1886, but lost heavily to the Liberals in the 1906 general election. The Liberals won 377 seats, while 54 LRC MPs were also elected – about half of these were **Lib-Labs**. The LRC was then renamed the **Labour Party**. There were also 83 Irish MPs who hoped to obtain Home Rule for Ireland, as this was supported by the Liberals.

- The Liberals, led by Campbell-Bannerman, were determined to push through **social**, **political** and **industrial** reforms. Asquith became Chancellor of the Exchequer, and Lloyd George became President of the Board of Trade. In 1908, Asquith became Prime Minister and Lloyd George took over as Chancellor.

- From **1906–09**, a number of important acts were passed:

  - Trade Disputes Act (1906) – this reversed the Taff Vale Decision

  - Workmen's Compensation Act (1906) – this gave industrial injuries compensation for those earning less than £250 a year

  - Schools Meals Act (1907) – this allowed Local Education Authorities (LEAs) to provide basic meals for children from poor families

  - Medical Inspection Act (1907) – this ordered LEAs to carry out regular medical inspections of school children

  - Children's Charter (1908) – this tried to protect children from begging and drinking alcohol, and set up Borstals so young criminals were not sent to adult prisons

  - Housing and Town Planning Act (1909) – this allowed local councils to demolish back-to-back housing and buy land for new housing developments.

Test yourself

1 Who was the first Liberal prime minister after the 1906 general election?

2 What do you understand by the term 'Lib-Labs'?

3 When did Lloyd George become Chancellor of the Exchequer?

Britain before the First World War, 1900–14

BBC GCSE Check and Test: History

Check the facts

- Some Liberal reforms were controversial. Most involved increased expenditure and so higher taxation.

> **One reform that was particularly expensive was the Old Age Pensions Act of 1908.**

190●

- For the first time, ordinary people who were too old to work would receive a pension of 5 shillings a week once they reached the age of 70, instead of going into the workhouse.

1914

- To pay for this, as well as other reforms, Lloyd George introduced the **People's Budget** in 1909. This mainly increased taxes on luxury items and the properties and incomes of the wealthiest people.

- When the Budget went to the unelected House of Lords (where the Conservatives had a huge majority), it was rejected. The Liberals called another election in January 1910. Although they won, it was a close result (Liberals: 275 seats; Tories: 273). Labour (40 seats) and the Irish Nationalists (82 seats) kept the Liberals in power.

- The 1909 Budget was reintroduced – the Lords passed it this time, but rejected the parliament bill, which proposed to limit the powers of the Lords. The Liberals called, and narrowly won, another election in December 1910. They said if the Lords did not pass the bill, the King had agreed to create enough Liberal peers (lords) to cancel the Tory majority.

- Rather than lose their Tory majority, the Lords accepted the bill. The Parliament Act, 1911, said the Lords could only delay a budget for one month and other bills for two years, provided the bills were passed three times by the Commons.

Test yourself

1 Why did the Lords object to the 1909 Budget?

2 How did the 1911 Parliament affect the powers of the hereditary House of Lords?

Check the facts

- During the nineteenth century, men gradually won the right to vote. Women remained without the vote. In 1897, the National Union of Women's Suffrage Societies **(NUWSS)** was set up by Millicent Fawcett. The organisation used peaceful methods of protest.

> **Members of the NUWSS were known as Suffragists.**

- Reforms after 1870 gave women greater equality, including, in 1880 and 1894, voting in local elections. However, women were still excluded from voting in general elections.

- In 1903, the Pankhursts formed the Women's Social and Political Union **(WSPU)**.

> **Members of the WSPU were known as Suffragettes. They were prepared to break the law to get the vote.**

- The Liberals gave women the right to stand in county council elections in 1906, but not the right to vote in general elections.

- From 1906, the WSPU became more **militant**. They heckled ministers, chained themselves to railings and smashed windows. Many of those arrested refused to pay fines and were sent to prison.

- In prison, many of the women went on hunger strike. From 1909, they were force-fed, which led to a public outcry. In 1912, the WSPU campaign became more violent, including arson attacks on postboxes. In 1913, Emily Davison was killed trying to stop the King's horse during the Derby.

- In 1913, the government passed the **Cat and Mouse Act**, which allowed female prisoners to be released for a time. They were rearrested and returned to prison once their strength had been restored by food.

- The WSPU stepped up its campaign at a time of major strikes and growing trouble in Ireland. However, when war broke out in 1914, the WSPU suspended its campaign.

Test yourself

1 What, respectively, do the initials NUWSS and WSPU stand for?

2 Who were the leaders of the WSPU?

3 What was the purpose of the 'Cat and Mouse' Act of 1913?

Britain before the First World War, 1900–14

BBC GCSE Check and Test: History

Britain, 1900–45

Britain before the First World War, 1900–14

Check the facts

- By the beginning of the twentieth century, the Liberal government faced a crisis in Ireland. It had long supported partial self-government for Ireland, but attempts to pass a **Home Rule Act** in 1886 and 1893 had failed to get through the British parliament.

> **The Conservatives were closely linked to the Unionists in Ireland, who wanted to remain directly ruled by Britain.**

- When the Liberals won in 1906, the Irish Nationalist MPs (who supported Home Rule and were led by Redmond) expected the Liberals to introduce another Home Rule Bill. They helped the Liberals in their struggles with the Lords in 1910. In return, they were promised Home Rule.

- The Third Home Rule Bill was introduced in 1912 and passed through the Commons. Although the Lords rejected the Bill, it would automatically become law in 1914 under the 1911 Parliament Act.

- Led by Carson, and supported by leading Conservatives, the Unionists formed a Solemn League and Covenant in 1912 to resist Home Rule.

> **The Unionists also set up the Ulster Volunteer Force, which soon had 100 000 armed members.**

- This worried the Nationalists and the **Sinn Fein** party, which had been formed in 1905. Those who wanted complete independence set up the **Irish Volunteers**. By 1914, the Irish Volunteers had 80 000 armed members. There was also the Irish Citizen Army, led by Connolly.

- In 1914, the '**Curragh Mutiny**' further alarmed the Nationalists, but then war broke out and the Home Rule Act was suspended until the end of the war.

Test yourself

1 Why was the Third Home Rule Bill of 1912 almost certain to become law?

2 What was the Solemn League and Covenant?

3 What was the 'Curragh Mutiny' of 1914?

190

191

Check the facts

900

- After the 1910 elections, the Liberals (dependent on Irish Nationalist and Labour Party MPs) became influenced by **New Liberalism**. They hoped this would limit Labour's rise.

- In 1911, the Parliament Act gave salaries to MPs (Labour MPs had no private incomes) and the Trade Union Act made it easier for trade unions to make donations to political parties (overturning the 1909 Osborne Judgement). The Liberals also passed acts to improve working conditions and pay (e.g. for miners and shopworkers).

914

> **New Liberalism reforms helped the beginning of a welfare state.**

- Especially important was the **National Insurance Act** of 1911, which established sickness and short-term unemployment benefits for most workers. These benefits were based on National Insurance contributions paid by the workers, the employers and the state.

- Although the Liberal government passed the Plural Voting Act in 1913, which stopped university graduates having two votes, women were still denied the vote.

- The Liberals were also faced with a wave of strikes in 1910–12, a time of unemployment and low pay. Violent confrontations took place between police and strikers – in some cases, the government sent in troops. Many trade unionists involved in the strikes were influenced by **syndicalist** ideas (the theory that factories and businesses should be owned and managed by the workers employed in them).

- In 1913, the three largest unions (the miners, transport workers and railway workers) formed the **Triple Industrial Alliance** to help workers against what they saw as cooperation between employers and the state. However, plans for a strike were called off when the First World War began.

Test yourself

1 How did the payment of MPs in 1911 help the Labour Party?

2 Why was the National Insurance Act of 1911 important?

Britain before the First World War, 1900–14

BBC GCSE Check and Test: History

Britain during the First World War, 1914–18

Check the facts

- When Britain declared war on Germany, thousands rushed to volunteer. Many thought it would be a short war ('over by Christmas'), while others saw it as a job (there were more volunteers in areas of high unemployment).

> **By September 1914, over 750 000 men had volunteered to fight.**

- The small **British Expeditionary Force** (BEF) that was sent over to help the French suffered heavy casualties. Some women (including the WSPU) encouraged men to enlist.

- The government began a campaign, headed by Lord Kitchener, to recruit 2.25 million men by October 1915. One way was to create **Pals Battalions**, by promising to keep together all volunteers from the same street, factory or town.

191

191

- As the war dragged on, the number of volunteers declined. So, in January 1916, **compulsory conscription** for all single men aged 18–41 was introduced by the Military Service Act. In March 1916, this was extended to married men.

- The medically unfit and those in 'essential' war jobs (such as mining and farming) were exempt.

- Some men refused to fight. They were conscientious objectors (known as **conchies** or **COs**).

> **There were 16 000 COs. Some objected on religious or moral grounds, others on political grounds.**

- Tribunals were set up to decide who were 'genuine' COs. About half agreed to do non-combatant work at the front; the rest refused and around 6000 were imprisoned. After the war, all COs were denied the vote for five years.

- In 1918, as the casualties continued to mount, the age limit for conscription was raised to 51.

Test yourself

1 Why was conscription introduced in 1916?

2 Who were the 'conchies'?

www.bbc.co.uk/revision

Check the facts

- To encourage men to enlist, untrue or exaggerated stories about the Germans were drawn up by the government's secret **War Propaganda Bureau** and were spread by the press (e.g. claiming that German troops ate Belgian babies or used dead bodies of British soldiers to make soap or cooking fats).

- People began to attack Germans who lived in Britain and, in 1915, the government interned all German males aged 17 to 45. Women, children and older men were forced to move to Germany.

> **Anti-German feelings ran so high that, in 1917, the King changed his family's German surname from Saxe-Coburg-Gotha to the more British-sounding Windsor.**

- The Battenberg family changed its surname to **Mountbatten** (Prince Louis of Battenberg, Britain's First Sea Lord, was forced to resign).

- Bad news was suppressed, while the true number of casualties was often hidden and successes exaggerated. In 1917, the National War Aims Committee was set up to hold rallies and issue leaflets to keep up morale. It was also designed to create a situation in which any anti-war sentiments would be deeply unpopular.

- People who tried to tell the truth – even soldiers – were punished and were often beaten up by those influenced by such propaganda.

- Poster campaigns were also launched to make civilians feel part of the war effort (e.g. asking people to eat less, do essential war work or carry out voluntary work).

Test yourself

1 What was the War Propaganda Bureau?

2 What was the propaganda that was issued by the British government and press designed to do?

Check the facts

- On 8 August 1914, the government rushed through the **Defence of the Realm Act** (DORA). This gave the government new and wide-ranging emergency powers to control the **Home Front**. Later that month, another DORA was passed that increased those powers. The government began to get involved in the economy and in people's lives more than ever before.

- **DORA** had four main aims:

  – to prevent spying
  – to defend against invasion
  – to increase war-production
  – to ensure there was enough food.

191 4

1918

- DORA allowed the government and the military to **censor** newspaper reports and films (via the Department of Information), along with letters sent home by soldiers. DORA also banned people from discussing military matters in public or spreading rumours – even the sale of binoculars was banned. Under DORA, people could be put in prison without trial, until 1915 when trial by jury was restored.

> **DORA allowed the government to take over any factory or workplace for war production.**

- A special Ministry of Munitions was set up to control weapons production. The government also took over the running (but not ownership) of ship-building, mining, transport and the railways.

- To boost production, DORA cut the opening hours of public houses to reduce drunkenness and absence from work. **British Summer Time** was introduced, giving an extra hour of daylight for farmworkers and others.

- However, the strain of long hours – and employers who tried to keep wages low – led to a number of strikes that meant production loss.

Test yourself

1 What was DORA?

2 How was the reduction in the opening hours of pubs meant to increase production?

Check the facts

- The First World War was the first 'total' war, shifting the front line to the Home Front in an attempt to break civilian morale. In November 1914, Great Yarmouth on the Norfolk coast was shelled by German ships. In December, three other east-coast towns were shelled. In Scarborough, 19 died and 80 were injured.

- However, from 1915, naval attacks were replaced by air raids. In January, King's Lynn and Yarmouth in Norfolk were the first British towns to be bombed by German **Zeppelins**.

- Zeppelins were huge airships, filled with hydrogen gas. Underneath was a cabin from which the crew dropped bombs – 20 Zeppelin raids on London killed 188 people.

> **In all, almost 2000 civilians were killed or injured in 51 Zeppelin raids on Britain from 1915–18.**

- By the end of 1916, the government had recruited over 17 000 people to protect civilians. Using searchlights, barrage (barrier) balloons, incendiary bullets and night fighters, a large number of Zeppelins were destroyed.

- DORA also allowed local military authorities to impose a **blackout**. This forced people to put out all lights if an air raid was expected.

- In 1917, the Germans switched to Gotha IV bomber planes.

> **The Gotha IV bomber planes killed or injured almost 3000 civilians in 57 raids.**

- In one raid on London, 162 people were killed. There was great fear, and many sheltered in the London Underground or in caves at Dover, which suffered most attacks. However, neither these nor the Zeppelin raids destroyed civilian morale, despite over 1500 deaths.

Test yourself

1 What were Zeppelins?

2 Name one way in which the government dealt with the threat posed by Zeppelin air raids.

Check the facts

- In 1916, there were serious food shortages in Britain as a result of the increasing attacks by **German U-boats** (submarines) on merchant shipping. By then, 4 per cent of British shipping, and neutral ships trading with Britain, had been sunk.

> **In 1917, the government introduced** voluntary rationing **to reduce food consumption and to distribute what there was more fairly.**

- People were asked to eat no more than $\frac{3}{4}$ lb of sugar, 4 lb of bread and $2\frac{1}{2}$ lb of meat a week.

191

191

- This failed, as poor people could not afford to buy even the amounts of sugar and meat permitted, while rich people simply bought extra on the **black market**.

- Under DORA, the government also turned public parks and other unused land into fields and allotments to grow extra food. Between 1914 and 1918, over 1.2 million hectares of such land were taken over. But the food shortages continued.

- In 1917, the German U-boat campaign was stepped up. By April 1917, it was claimed that Britain had only six weeks' food supply left. In 1918, full-scale compulsory rationing was introduced. Because this system worked reasonably well, the diets of many poor people were better than they had been in 1914.

- Lord Devonport became Food Controller and organised a successful increase in wheat and potato production. Despite this, the reduced intake of food for many during the war left them vulnerable to the flu epidemic that hit Europe in 1918 – almost 230 000 British people died.

Test yourself

1 Why did the rationing introduced in 1917 fail?

2 When did rationing become compulsory?

Check the facts

- With so many men at the front, serious labour shortages arose – these gaps were filled by women.

> **Especially important were those women who worked in munitions (armaments) factories. There were about 900 000 'munitionettes' by 1918.**

- During the 1915 **shell shortage** crisis, Lloyd George financed a march led by Mrs Pankhurst that called on employers to take on more women workers.

- Many women worked in engineering factories or became conductors on trams and buses, while over 400 000 became clerks and secretaries – before 1914, these had been mainly male occupations.

- Many others joined the **Women's Land Army** to carry out farm work or the **Voluntary Aid Detachments** (VADs). Most VAD jobs were traditional women's work, such as laundresses, cooks, maids and nurses. However, a few VADs worked as ambulance drivers or motorbike messengers at the front.

- Other women joined the **First Aid Nursing Yeomanry** (FANY) or one of the women's military units formed in 1917–18 **(WAAC, WRNS or WRAF)**. Most acted as cooks or clerks, while some became drivers or welders.

- Many women, including the Suffragettes, also joined campaigns that encouraged men to enlist.

> **Some Suffragettes gave out white feathers (a sign of cowardice) to young men in civilian clothes.**

- At the end of the war, most women lost their jobs (Pre-War Practices Act, 1919) and returned to their traditional roles. However, in 1918, women over the age of 30 were at last given the vote.

Test yourself

1 Who were the 'munitionettes'?

2 What kind of jobs were done by the VAD units?

3 Why did most women lose their wartime jobs after 1918?

Check the facts

- To pay for the war, Britain had to increase taxation, raise loans and sell 25 per cent of overseas assets. By 1918, Britain had a debt of £10 billion and much trade had been lost, especially to the USA and Japan.

- Long-term problems with many British industries were made worse by the war – especially the 'staple' industries of coal, iron and steel. By 1920, loss of wartime contracts and demobilisation had resulted in a slump.

> **By 1921, there were over 2 million unemployed.**

- Although trade revived a little, unemployment never dropped below a million before 1939.

- To deal with long-term unemployment, an **Unemployment Insurance Act** in 1921 allowed payment of uninsured benefit.

1918

> **This payment was known as the dole.**

- Acts passed in 1927 and 1929, however, reduced both benefits and their duration.

- Before the War, Lloyd George had promised soldiers a **'fit country for heroes'**. Mass conscription had revealed poor diets, bad housing and lack of education.

- In 1918, the Education Act raised the school leaving age to 14 and introduced medical inspections for secondary school pupils. The Addison Housing Act, 1919, planned to build 200 000 new **council houses** to replace the slums, which were to be cleared.

1939

- In 1918, women over 30 years old received the vote and the right to stand as MPs. However, women did not receive equal voting rights to men until 1928, when all those over 21 could vote.

Test yourself

1 How did the cost of the First World War affect the British economy?

2 When did women achieve equal voting rights to men?

Check the facts

- During the First World War, trade unionists had benefitted from government control of wages, prices and industries. In 1919–20, a number of strikes resulted in wage increases in line with price rises.

- However, the post-war slump made employers keen to regain control of their companies and reduce wages.

> **High unemployment meant it was more difficult to have successful strikes.**

- Particular problems existed in coal mining. Although the majority of a Commission of Inquiry recommended **nationalisation** (government ownership) of the mines, the government decided to end government control in March 1921.

- The mine owners immediately announced wage cuts. A planned **Triple Industrial Alliance** strike for 15 April failed when the railway workers withdrew **(Black Friday)**.

- Another serious crisis hit in 1925 – again, mine owners demanded wage cuts, along with an increase in hours in the working day. The Triple Industrial Alliance was revived and, in July, the government gave the mine owners a subsidy (to last until April 1926) to prevent wage cuts **(Red Friday)**.

- The Samuel Commission was set up to look into the problems of mining. At the same time, the government made plans for dealing with a major strike, including the semi-official OMS.

- When the subsidy ended, the owners insisted on the wage cuts. The miners persuaded the TUC to call a General Strike in May, but called it off nine days later.

- The Trade Disputes Act of 1927 made all general and **sympathy** strikes illegal, and many strikers were sacked.

Test yourself

1 How had workers benefitted from government control of the economy during the war?

2 What was 'Red Friday'?

3 What was the OMS?

Check the facts

- While most Irishmen (Catholic and Protestant) joined the army, a minority of **Republicans** (who wanted more than what the Home Rule Act of 1914 had to offer) saw the war as an opportunity for gaining independence.

- In Dublin, on Easter Monday 1916, about two thousand Irish Volunteers and members of the Irish Citizen Army proclaimed the **Independence of Ireland**. After six days of fighting, the survivors of the **Easter Rebellion** surrendered – 15 were executed for treason.

- This turned the rebels into national heroes and support for Sinn Fein grew.

> **In the 1918 elections, Sinn Fein won 73 out of Ireland's 105 seats. Led by de Valera, they set up their own parliament (Dail Eireann).**

1918

- A guerrilla **War of Independence** then began between the IRA and the British army. The British used ten thousand special troops (the '**Black and Tans**' and Auxilliaries).

> **In 1920, Britain passed the Government of Ireland Act, dividing Ireland into Northern Ireland and the Irish Free State in the south.**

- By 1921, stalemate led to a truce.

- A majority of Sinn Fein accepted the partition of Ireland in 1922, but a minority (led by de Valera) rejected it and resigned from the Free State government. A civil war then broke out between the pro-Treaty and the anti-Treaty groups. The pro-Treaty forces won in 1923.

1939

- In 1926, de Valera formed Fianna Fail, which won the 1932 elections. He reduced British powers and, in 1937, the south was renamed **Eire**.

Test yourself

1 Who was the leader of Sinn Fein in 1918?

2 Why did a civil war break out in the Irish Free State in 1922?

Check the facts

- After the **General Strike** in 1926, the British economy benefitted from an improvement in world trade and unemployment dropped to a million. In the 1929 election, the Labour Party (for the first time) won the largest number of seats and formed its second minority goverment, with **MacDonald** as prime minister.

> **When the Wall Street Crash in the USA triggered off the Great Depression, British exports fell by almost 50 per cent and unemployment rose to over 3 million.**

- Although more had to be paid out in unemployment benefits, tax revenues began to decline as so many people were now without jobs.

- Early suggestions to help the unemployed were opposed by Treasury civil servants and the Conservatives. By 1931, Britain was in a serious **economic crisis**.

- When the USA called in loans made to Germany, Britain loaned Germany (and Austria) £200 million to prevent their total collapse, which would have hit British exports further. At the same time, an extra £30 million was borrowed by the British government to help pay unemployment benefits.

- Such actions led to increased criticism. In 1931, MacDonald set up the May Committee to report on the crisis and to make suggestions.

- The Report (which did not come out until August, when Parliament had broken up for the summer) recommended huge cuts in benefits, the wages of public servants and government spending. The USA, which had already loaned Britain £100 million, refused to lend more until huge cuts in government spending were made.

Test yourself

1 What was the Wall Street Crash in October 1929?

2 What did the May Committee recommend in 1931?

BBC GCSE Check and Test: History

Check the facts

- MacDonald and Snowden, the Chancellor, reluctantly agreed to the cuts recommended by the May Committee, including a 10 per cent cut in unemployment benefit. However, most of the other Labour ministers, and the Labour Party itself, were opposed to the cuts.

- This resulted in MacDonald's **resignation** as prime minister. However, instead of a new election being called, the King asked MacDonald to form a coalition national government to include the leading members of the other two parties.

> **MacDonald agreed to lead a new National Government. It was supported by the Conservative Party and most of the Liberal Party.**

1918

- The Labour Party and most of its MPs were against the idea – they now became the **Opposition**. MacDonald and his Labour supporters in the Commons were seen as traitors and were later expelled from the party.

> **The new National Government took over in September 1931.**

- The National Government immediately introduced an emergency **supplementary** budget. This raised the rates of various taxes and reduced allowances and exemptions to increase government income.

- The National Government also passed an Act to cut the salaries of public officials and employees by 15 per cent. At the same time, all benefits were cut by 10 per cent, the duration of benefits was reduced and National Insurance contributions were increased.

1939

- The National Government also took Britain 'off the Gold Standard' By ending the link between the British pound and the value of a fixed amount of gold (and the US dollar), British exports became cheaper. This was to revive trade and reduce unemployment.

Test yourself

1 Which political party was most in favour of the formation of a National Government in 1931?

2 How did the Labour Party react to MacDonald's new government?

Check the facts

- In October 1931, MacDonald called an election – the National Government **candidates** won a large majority, but most were National Conservative MPs.
- After the 1935 election, which the National Government also won (though with a reduced majority), MacDonald resigned and was replaced by **Stanley Baldwin**, the Conservative leader.

> **The National Government decided to put higher import duties (tariffs) on certain foreign products.**

- This was known as **protectionism**, as it tried to protect British manufacturers from foreign competition.
- Snowden, the Chancellor, was opposed, as he feared other countries would retaliate and British exports would suffer even more.
- Snowden resigned and was replaced by **Neville Chamberlain** (also a Conservative).

> **In 1932, Chamberlain brought in the Import Duties Act. This act put a 10 per cent duty on all foreign goods.**

- In 1932, the National Government gave state subsidies to railway companies and financed public work schemes in the most distressed areas. This aid policy was increased by the Depressed Areas Act, 1934, which spent about £2 million a year in these **Special Areas**. In 1934, Chamberlain reduced income tax.
- In 1934, the Unemployment Insurance Act set up the Unemployment Assistance Board to deal with extra payments to the unemployed. Although the 1931 benefit cuts were partly restored, a means test was introduced.

> **The unemployed resented the introduction of a means test. In the worst hit areas, there were hunger marches. The most famous was the Jarrow Crusade in 1936.**

- During this period, slum clearance continued, although more private houses than council houses were built. In 1937, Chamberlain became prime minister.

Test yourself

1 Which party dominated the National Government in the period 1931–40?
2 Why did the Unemployment Insurance Act of 1934 anger many of the unemployed?

BBC GCSE Check and Test: History

Check the facts

- Before the Second World War began in September 1939, Britain had already started to make war preparations, because of the growing threat posed by Nazi Germany.

- After Nazi Germany's invasion of the rest of Czechoslovakia in March 1938, Britain and France signed a treaty with Poland.

> **In April, the British government introduced** conscription. **This was the first time it had been implemented in peacetime. The** Military Training Act **called up all men aged 20 to 21.**

- In September 1939, the call-up was extended to all men aged 19 to 41. Later that same year it was widened to include 18-year-olds. However, in the early stages, the call-up was criticised for being slow.

- Over a million men volunteered for military service or asked for their call-up to be speeded up. Many believed **Fascism** was an evil that had to be fought and had been highly critical of appeasement.

- There was also a more thought-out system of recruitment than in the previous war. A **Schedule of Reserved Occupations** had been drawn up, and employers in war-related industries could ask for the call-up of specialist workers to be deferred. This avoided the skilled labour shortages that had caused problems at the start of the First World War.

- In 1940, as the fear of invasion increased, all men who had not been called up were recruited into the **Local Defence Volunteers**. By the end of June 1940, there were over 1.5 million volunteers. In July, they were renamed the **Home Guard**.

193

Test yourself

194

1 Why was the call-up of some men deferred?

2 What role was the Home Guard supposed to play?

Check the facts

- As in the First World War, the British government used **censorship** and **propaganda** to safeguard military information and to keep up civilian morale during the Second World War.

> The **Censorship Bureau** banned all newspaper photographs of wounded soldiers, dead air-raid victims and houses destroyed by enemy bombing.

- Because of the existence of spies, the government ran poster campaigns, such as the **Careless Talk Costs Lives** campaign.

- However, the radio broadcasts from Nazi Germany by **Lord Haw-Haw** were not banned, and the BBC was not taken over.

- Comedy and musical programmes on the radio helped to keep up morale. By 1945, over 10 million homes had radio licences, which meant about 25 million people could listen to broadcasts.

- Cinemas played documentaries and news films that showed Allied successes. There were also feature films that showed either all Britons working together to win the war or glorified past British victories from earlier times.

- The government ran campaigns to make everyone feel like they were part of the war effort (e.g. **Your Britain – Fight For It Now**, **Is Your Journey Really Necessary?**, **Dig For Victory**). Churchill and other ministers made regular radio broadcasts urging people to 'do their bit'.

- The Ministry of Information also issued propaganda to help maintain morale. Particularly important was how it turned the defeat at Dunkirk into a 'victory'. Soon everyone was talking about the **'Dunkirk spirit'**. During the **Battle of Britain**, German aircraft losses were exaggerated.

939

945

Test yourself

1 Which government body was responsible for ensuring that newspapers did not publish photographs that might reduce civilian morale?

2 How did the Ministry of Information deal with incidents such as Dunkirk and the Battle of Britain?

BBC GCSE Check and Test: History

Check the facts

- After the fall of France in June 1940, Hitler offered peace to Britain, but Churchill rejected his peace terms. Hitler then ordered the invasion of Britain (**Operation Sealion**).

> **The first stage of the** Battle of Britain **began in July, when the German** Luftwaffe **bombed merchant shipping in the Channel.**

- In August, they tried to destroy radar stations, airfields and RAF Fighter Command.
- The RAF fought back and, at first, was able to offer an effective response. However, by early September, the RAF's losses were greater than the number of new planes being produced.
- Then, just at the critical moment, Hitler ordered the Luftwaffe to begin night bombing of London (**the Blitz**).

> **By the time the** Luftwaffe **resumed its attacks on Fighter Command, the RAF was in a much stronger position, as factories had produced almost 2000 fighters in four months.**

- Large numbers of German bombers and fighters were destroyed and, in the end, the Luftwaffe failed to win control of the skies.
- The government and press exaggerated the number of German planes shot down by the 'few'. It also emphasised the role of the **Spitfire**, when, in fact, the **Hurricane** was used much more.

Date	RAF figs 1940	RAF figs after the war	Official Luftwaffe figs
15 Aug	185	76	55
18 Aug	155	71	49
15 Sept	185	56	50
27 Sept	153	55	42
TOTAL	**678**	**258**	**196**

The number of German planes destroyed over four days during the Battle of Britain

- At the end of September 1940, Hitler postponed his plans for the invasion of Britain. But until June 1941, Britain was still without an ally.

Test yourself

1 Why was Hitler's decision to order the Luftwaffe to bomb London in early September so important?

2 What can you learn from the two different sets of figures given by the RAF on German losses during the Battle of Britain?

1939

1945

Check the facts

- Fear of the impact of bombing raids on civilian morale had contributed to the **policy of appeasement**. During the Czech Crisis in 1938, the British government had issued **gas masks**. When war was declared in 1939, it issued them once again.

- The government took several other steps to protect civilians: barrage balloons, searchlights, anti-aircraft batteries and air-raid shelters (the **Anderson** and the **Morrison**). By 1945, over 500 000 shelters had been provided).

- **Air-Raid Precautions** (ARP) wardens had been recruited in 1937. By 1939, there were almost 500 000. The wardens patrolled the streets, enforced the **black-out** regulations, helped people to shelters and gave help after air raids.

- The first air raids of **the Blitz** began in September 1940, when London was bombed. The raids continued until May 1941. Other major cities were also bombed, including Liverpool, Manchester and Norwich.

- It was not only the docks, factories and railways that were bombed. Civilian housing was also deliberately targeted. In London, many people occupied the Underground stations. In other cities, civilians trekked out to the countryside each night. However, most used the official shelters.

- Although the bombing raids declined after 1941, a new danger emerged in 1944 and 1945: the **V1** and **V2** attacks. Damage to factories was limited and did little to slow vital war production.

> **In all, over 60 000 civilians were killed in the Blitz and over 250 000 homes destroyed.**

- Although there was some loss of morale at first, most were determined to resist.

Test yourself

1 Which group of people were responsible for enforcing the 'black-out' regulations?

2 When did the regular bombing of the Blitz come to an end?

3 What were (i) the V1s (ii) the V2s?

Evacuation and rationing

Check the facts

- The British government evacuated children from high-risk bombing areas. In September 1939, almost 1.5 million children were evacuated, along with mothers, pregnant women and teachers.

- However, almost half the parents kept their children at home. During the **Phoney War** (September 1939 to April 1940), many parents brought their evacuated children home.

> **Once the Blitz started, evacuation began again. By 1941, over 3 million had been evacuated.**

- As in the last war, German U-boat attacks led to food shortages. Until 1943, British merchant-shipping losses were high and food imports were down 50 per cent.

> **In January 1940, rationing began of those foods in short supply.**

- People registered with their usual shops and were given ration books – these had **coupons** to exchange for set amounts of foods. At the end of 1941, all tinned foods were rationed.

- The government also ran campaigns to increase food production and avoid waste. The **Dig for Victory** campaign encouraged people to dig up lawns and parks. By the end of 1942, the number of allotments had doubled to almost 1.5 million.

- Soap, shoes and clothes were rationed. There was a **Make-Do-and-Mend** campaign, while the use of petrol was discouraged by the **Is Your Journey Really Necessary?** campaign.

- The situation improved after 1943, when Germany began to lose the Battle of the Atlantic.

193!

194!

Test yourself

1 Why did many mothers bring their evacuated children back during the 'Phoney War'?

2 When was rationing introduced in the Second World War?

Check the facts

- Women played an important role in the war effort. In September 1939, they were encouraged to volunteer for one of the women's sections of the armed forces or to do essential war work.

> **In 1941, all single women aged 19 to 30 were conscripted and had to choose one of these options.**

- By 1943, over 7 million women were involved in the war effort. Fifty per cent of women aged 14 to 59 did some form of war service. This, plus government control of 75 per cent of industry, resulted in industrial production being eight times higher in 1943 than in 1939.

- Many women worked in munitions factories or factories producing other vital war supplies. Others drove lorries and buses or worked on the railways. Before the war, these had been 'male only' occupations.

- About 30 000 women were in the **Women's Land Army**, carrying out agricultural work. Others worked in offices – especially the Civil Service and the Post Office – while some joined voluntary organisations such as the **WVS** (Women's Voluntary Service).

- There were also about 500 000 women in the three women's armed services. While most did office work or worked as drivers, some ATA members flew newly produced planes from the factories to air bases and some WRNS radio mechanics flew to test new equipment.

- Women in the ATS also worked on anti-aircraft batteries or as nurses.

- Although women in the three armed services were not allowed to take part in combat, some women members of the **SOE** (Special Operations Executive) did – mostly as secret agents in France.

Test yourself

1 Which group of women were conscripted for war work in 1941?

2 What was unusual about the role played by women members of the SOE?

THE FIRST WORLD WAR, 1914–19

01 The start of the First World War
1 (a) Russia (b) Turkey.
2 Defeat France before Russia mobilised, to avoid a two-front war.
3 Belgian resistance/Russia already mobilised, so some troops were diverted to the east.

02 Stalemate
1 When both sides tried to capture the Channel ports.
2 Each side copied the other's inventions.
3 To wear down the enemy by destoying more of their men than they do of yours.

03 The trenches
1 A = Communication trench.
  B = Reserve trench.
2 (i) Attacking over the top of the trenches (ii) The area between the opposing front-line trenches.
3 Two from: trench foot/gangrene/shell-shock/frostbite/lice.
4 They were punished (even executed) for cowardice.

04 New technology
1 Chlorine/phosgene/mustard.
2 They broke down; got stuck in the mud; the heat inside made soldiers ill.
3 Serious food shortages in Britain, because so many supply ships were sunk.
4 Use of convoy system/zig-zag sailing patterns/hydrophones.
5 Poor navigation/they were difficult to control in bad weather/British counter methods (searchlights, barrage balloons, incendiary bullets).

05 Other fronts
1 Austria–Hungary/Germany.
2 (i) Weaken Turkey/get supplies to Russia (ii) Defend British oil supplies in Middle East.

06 End of the stalemate
1 Russia withdrew/the USA joined.
2 Defeat the Allies before extra US troops arrived/end the war before the situation in Germany deteriorated.
3 There was no overall plan/they advanced too quickly/insufficient supplies of reserves, food and equipment/use of tanks by Allies/arrival of US troops.

07 Wilson's Fourteen Points and the Big Three
1 Britain, France, USA.
2 (i) Lloyd George (ii) Clemenceau.
3 To repair damaged land, railways and industries/to keep Germany weak.

08 Problems of peacemaking
1 Workers' uprisings and mutinies/the kaiser had fled.
2 Austria–Hungary.
3 Near starvation in Germany/economic collapse.

09 The Treaty of Versailles
1 They were taken over by Britain, France and Japan (under League of Nations' mandates).
2 Two from: Alsace–Lorraine, Upper Silesia, West Prussia, Posen, Eupen–Malmédy, North Schleswig.
3 Union between Germany and Austria.

10 The German reaction
1 They were not present during the discussions/they were given an ultimatum – sign or fight.
2 Article 231 forced Germany to accept total blame for causing the war.
3 Because other states had also helped start the war/because they had to pay massive compensation (reparations) as a result.

11 The other treaties
1 It was split into new states – and Austria–Hungary became two separate countries.
2 The new countries formed as a result of the break-up of the Austro–Hungarian empire.
3 Two from: Czechoslovakia, Yugoslavia, Poland.

12 Assessment of the treaties
1 Disrupted trade and the economy of a large region.
2 A communist revolution had broken out, led by Bela Kun.
3 The nationalist leader who came to power in Turkey.

THE LEAGUE OF NATIONS, 1919–39

13 Organisation
1 The Fourteen Points.
2 Prevent war/bring about general disarmament.
3 Improve worldwide health, education, working conditions.
4 Powers/actions to make countries comply with League decisions.

14 Weaknesses
1 It was the strongest power in the world.
2 Britain and France were seen as the victors/these two countries often differed on important issues.

15 Successes in the 1920s
1 Two from: Upper Silesia, 1921 (Poland v. Germany)/Aaland Islands, 1921 (Finland v. Sweden)/Greece's invasion of Bulgaria, 1925.
2 Attempts were blocked by Britain in 1923.
3 Germany was allowed to join the League in 1926/special commissions did good work on war refugees, health and disease, slave labour, working conditions.

16 Failures in the 1920s
1 The Conference of Ambassadors gave Vilna to Poland.
2 France, one of the main members of the League, did not consult it.
3 The Corfu Incident.

17 Successes in the 1930s
1 Colombia v. Peru.
2 These were small/weak countries.
3 Governments became more aggressive to solve problems/countries reluctant to impose sanctions in case more trade lost.

18 Failures in the 1930s
1 The failure to agree 'equal treatment' for Germany led Hitler to take Germany out of the Conference and the League.
2 The League took no firm action/sanctions were ignored or imposed too late/the aggressors just left the League.

RUSSIA IN REVOLUTION, 1917–41

19 Tsarist Russia
1 One from: general poverty/desire for reforms/defeats in the Russo-Japanese War, 1904–05/'Bloody Sunday'.
2 The Tsar promised a Duma (parliament) and free speech.
3 He dismissed Dumas that criticised him or that had too many liberals and radicals; gave them very little power; and, in 1912, he went back to ruling without one.

20 War and the March Revolution
1 Land reform for peasants.
2 One from: heavy military defeats/bad military leadership and lack of weapons, etc./lack of food and fuel in towns/influence of Rasputin.
3 Dual Authority/shared power between the Provisional Government and the Petrograd Soviet.

21 The Bolsheviks and the November Revolution
1 'Peace, Bread and Land'; 'All Power o the Soviets'.
2 The Petrograd Soviet.
3 Leon Trotsky.
4 Left Social Revolutionaries.

22 The Civil War
1 Treaty of Brest–Litovsk, 1918.
2 The Reds were united/Reds had control of the centre (railways and factories)/Trotsky built up large and efficient Red Army/peasants opposed Whites as wanted to keep landlords' lands/many resented foreign intervention on the side of the Whites.

23 War Communism
1 To keep the Red Army and factory workers supplied with food and equipment.
2 They hid surplus food and grew less.

24 The NEP
1 Because it involved a partial return to capitalism.
2 (i) Rich peasants (ii) Private traders.

25 Lenin's 'Testament'
1 General-Secretary of the CPSU.
2 That Stalin should be dismised from all his positions.

BBC GCSE Check and Test: History

26 The power struggle
1 Commissar for War.
2 The combined forces of Trotsky's Left Opposition, and Zinoviev and Kamenev and their supporters.
3 Stalin's decision to end the NEP.

27 Collectivisation
1 State collective farms.
2 They killed their animals/destroyed crops and equipment/killed communist officials.

28 The Five-Year Plans
1 He feared invasion/wanted to weaken the kulaks and nepmen/wanted to make the USSR more socialist.
2 Steel, iron, coal, oil and electrical industries – all needed before industrialisation can begin.
3 116 million tonnes.

29 The Great Purge
1 The popular party boss of Leningrad.
2 The public trials where Communist leaders who opposed Stalin were forced to admit their 'guilt' of 'crimes' against the USSR.
3 20 per cent of all officers were killed, including many of the highest ranking ones.

30 Stalin's foreign policy
1 Hitler came to power – his policies were to get 'Living Space' in the east and destroy communism.
2 One from: gain extra time for building up Soviet defences/use Poland as a buffer zone when attacked.

GERMANY, 1918–45

31 Impact of the First World War
1 Unemployed right-wing German ex-soldiers.
2 They were captured and murdered.

32 The Weimar Republic
1 The power to rule by decree and to suspend the Constitution.
2 The system of PR gave seats to many small parties, so no party had an overall majority.

33 Early problems
1 They did nothing to help the government – attempted putsch was defeated by workers going on strike.
2 Germany had not paid its second reparations instalment.

34 The birth of the Nazi Party
1 1921.
2 Unemployed ex-soldiers and others (Brownshirts) who attacked leftwing groups.
3 November 1923.

35 Stresemann and the 'Golden Years'
1 Called off passive resistance and issued a new currency (the Rentenmark).
2 Gave Germany loans, reduced reparations payments and gave Germany more time to pay.

36 The Nazis' 'Lean Years'
1 *Mein Kampf* ('My Struggle').
2 It had been banned after 1923 and had split into factions.
3 Hitler's elite bodyguard (Blackshirts).

37 Depression and the rise of the Nazis
1 Ended US loans, and earlier ones had to be repaid.
2 July 1932.
3 30 January 1933.

38 Establishing Nazi control
1 It suspended the Constitution, and gave Hitler the power to rule by decree for four years.
2 The SS murdered Rohm and other SA leaders.
3 Minister of Propaganda and Culture.

39 The Nazi economy
1 One of: the National Labour Service was extended/public works programmes/rearmament contracts/communists, Jews and women were forced out of jobs/conscription.
2 Get Germany ready for war by 1940.

40 Women and young people
1 They were excluded from state jobs/employers were encouraged to only employ men/loans and medals were given to those who stayed at home and had babies.
2 Racism, on how 'Aryans' were superior, while others (Jews, Slavs, gypsies, blacks) were inferior.

41 The Holocaust
1 The Nuremburg Laws.
2 The 'Final Solution' – the extermination of all Jews.

42 Opposition
1 The Swing/the Eidelweiss Pirates/the Meuten.
2 Gave out leaflets/wrote anti-Nazi slogans/held anti-Nazi demonstrations.

THE USA, 1919–45

43 Isolationism
1 The Democrats.
2 November 1918.
3 Those who had come from northern Europe (White Anglo-Saxon Protestants).

44 The Republican 'Boom'
1 Governments not getting involved/controlling private enterprise – 'leaving it alone'.
2 The car industry.

45 Prohibition and gangsters
1 Because of its associations with poverty, drunkenness and absence from work, links to violence and crime.
2 Illegal bars where alcohol was available.
3 It had given criminal gangs the chance to grow rich/many officials and police had become corrupt/many ordinary people were prepared to break this law.

46 Intolerance in the USA
1 Ku Klux Klan.
2 When wealthy Americans and the police began a campaign against left-wing and radical organisations and individuals.

47 The Wall Street Crash
1 60 per cent.
2 October 1929.

48 Hoover and the Depression
1 Herbert Hoover.
2 Laissez-faire and 'rugged individualism'.
3 Veteran soldiers who marched to the White House to demand early payment of their war pensions.

49 Roosevelt and the New Deal
1 In March 1933.
2 Radio talks to increase confidence and tell Americans what he was going to do to help them.
3 These were the various New Deal agencies set up by Roosevelt.

50 Opposition to the New Deal
1 Government interference/increased taxation/greater rights for workers (e.g. to join trade unions).
2 They ruled many of them 'unconstitutional'.
3 He was not doing enough to help the poor.

51 Success of the New Deal
1 There was a new decline in world trade/Roosevelt had reduced government spending as he thought the Depression was over.
2 Rearmament and then entry into the Second World War.

52 US foreign policy
1 Latin America and Asia/the Pacific.
2 Japan.
3 These said the USA should not get involved in other countries' disputes (e.g. selling weapons to one side or the other).

THE SECOND WORLD WAR, 1939–45

53 Growing tensions, 1930–35
1 1933.
2 Mussolini was angry at Britain and France's response over his invasion of Abyssinia/the Anglo-German Naval Treaty angered France.

54 Hitler's actions, 1936–8
1 He ordered the reoccupation of the Rhineland.
2 The agreement between Mussolini and Hitler to become allies.
3 Mussolini was no longer opposed to this (in 1934, he had joined Britain and France to stop this – they had then formed the Stresa Front).

55 Appeasement and the Czech Crisis
1 The prime ministers of France and Britain.
2 It contained the Czech border defences and armaments works.

56 From Czechoslovakia to Poland

1 The invasion of the rest of Czechoslovakia.
2 Time to build up Soviet defences/ a buffer zone on Polish territory.

57 The 'Phoney War' and Blitzkrieg

1 'Lightning War' – a rapid advance based on aircraft, tanks and paratroopers.
2 22 June 1940.

58 Operation Barbarossa and the Eastern Front

1 22 June 1941.
2 Stalingrad.

59 Battle of the Atlantic

1 When the US loaned military equipment to Britain.
2 To defeat the German U-boat campaign, which was preventing food and supplies getting to Britain.
3 Germany's secret radio codes were broken.

60 North Africa and Italy

1 The Suez Canal was a vital shipping route.
2 El Alamein.
3 Allowed the launch of 'Operation Torch', which led to Allied control of North Africa – this then led to the invasion of Italy.

61 War in Asia and the Pacific

1 Banned the sale of oil, iron and aircraft to Japan/froze all Japanese assets in the USA.
2 To establish a Japanese empire in SE Asia, and so gain supplies of oil and other raw materials.
3 Where US forces ignored smaller islands held by Japan, and instead concentrated on the strategically more important ones.

62 D-Day and A-bombs

1 Take pressure off the USSR, which was facing the bulk of the German army.
2 The invasion of Nazi-held Europe: D-Day.
3 US forces had captured many airfields near to Japan by then.

SUPERPOWER RELATIONS SINCE 1945

63 Origins of the Cold War

1 A country so strong economically and militarily that it can dominate a region or even the world.
2 The struggle between capitalism and socialism/communism.
3 The fact it had been invaded three times from the west since 1900/the earlier policy of appeasement and the delay in opening up a second front/the US nuclear monopoly.

64 Conferences, 1943–5

1 Churchill and Stalin.
2 Truman was more hostile to the Soviet Union/communism.

65 Early tensions

1 The USA refused to share its nuclear technology.
2 To obtain friendly governments/a buffer zone, so that there would be less risk of invasion in the future.
3 The invisible border separating the capitalist West from the communist East.

66 The Truman Doctrine and the Marshall Plan

1 Kennan's assessment that the Soviet Union was determined to expand.
2 Not to allow any more countries to 'go communist'/move out of the USA's sphere of influence.
3 Rebuild the economies of western Europe (especially Germany)/prevent poverty in Europe leading to the growth of communism/weaken Soviet control of east Europe/help the US economy expand in Europe.

67 The 'Iron Curtain' and the Berlin Blockade

1 The great destruction done by the Germans and the 'scorched earth' policy/the USSR had suffered more than other countries/fears of US plans to rebuild Germany after the war.
2 The three western zones of Germany, after the USA, Britain and France had agreed to merge them into one economic zone, without consulting the USSR.
3 They organised the Berlin Airlift.

68 Alliances and the Arms Race
1 January 1949.
2 The Warsaw Pact.
3 August 1949.

69 The Korean War
1 Communists took control of China in October 1949.
2 The USSR was absent from the Security Council (in protest at the USA's refusal to allow Communist China a seat at the UN), and so could not use its veto.
3 July 1953.

70 Hungary and the Berlin Wall
1 1955.
2 Nagy's decision to take Hungary out of the Warsaw Pact.

71 Cuba and the Missile Crisis
1 Latin America and the Caribbean.
2 The USA had helped to plan and equip the Bay of Pigs invasion attempt.
3 Khrushchev agreed to withdraw Soviet missiles; in return, the US gave a private promise not to invade Cuba and to remove their missiles in Turkey.

72 The Vietnam War
1 Elections for reunification.
2 Communists in South Vietnam who formed a guerrilla force.
3 Massive US bombing of North Vietnam.
4 1973.

73 Détente
1 A relaxing/easing of tensions and the arms race between the USA and the Soviet Union.
2 Nixon/Carter.

74 Czechoslovakia and Poland
1 Alexander Dubcek.
2 Announcement by Brezhnev after the invasion of Czechoslovakia – that no East European state could leave the Warsaw Pact or introduce a multi-party system.
3 1981.

75 The 'Second' Cold War
1 Afghanistan.
2 Reagan.
3 He claimed the USA had fallen behind the USSR in the nuclear arms race.

76 The end of the Cold War
1 (i) Intermediate-range (medium) missiles were reduced. (ii) Long-range missiles were reduced.
2 1990.
3 December 1991.

BRITAIN, 1900–45

77 Britain in 1900
1 For markets/raw materials/larger armies.
2 1900.

78 Liberal reforms, 1906–11
1 Campbell-Bannerman.
2 Working-class men who, before, had been supporters or MPs of the Liberal Party.
3 1908.

79 Opposition
1 Increased taxes on the landed properties and incomes of the wealthiest people.
2 They could only delay budgets for one month; and other bills for two years, provided they had been passed by the Commons three times.

80 The Suffragettes
1 National Union of Women's Suffrage Societies/Women's Social and Political Union.
2 Mrs Pankhurst and her daughters Christabel and Sylvia.
3 Dealing with Suffragette hunger strikers in prison.

81 Ireland
1 Because of the 1911 Parliament Act, the Lords could no longer block it.
2 An agreement signed by Protestants in Ulster to oppose Home Rule.
3 When army officers in Ireland were allowed to temporarily resign their commissions, rather than enforce Home Rule after it became law.

82 Liberal reforms after 1911
1 Before, MPs needed a private income – having a salary meant ordinary working people could become MPs.
2 Most workers were covered for sickness and short-term unemployment benefits for the first time – the start of the Welfare State.

Answers

83 Recruitment and opposition
1 The high casualty rates/the number of volunteers was falling.
2 Conscientious Objectors – those who refused to fight in the war.

84 Propaganda
1 A government body that spread false stories about German 'cruelty'.
2 To keep up morale/make anti-war sentiments unpopular.

85 DORA
1 The Defence of the Realm Act – that gave the government wide emergency powers.
2 To reduce drunkenness, which led to absence from work.

86 Air raids
1 Large German airships used to bomb British towns.
2 Barrage balloons/searchlights/incendiary bullets/night fighters.

87 Rationing
1 It was voluntary – the poor couldn't afford to buy the suggested amounts of food, while the rich simply bought extra on the 'black market'.
2 1918.

88 The role of women
1 Women who worked in the munitions/armaments factories.
2 Cooks/laundresses/maids/nurses/drivers of ambulances and motorbikes.
3 The Pre-War Practices Act, 1919, forced employers to sack women and employ men returned from the army.

89 Impact of the First World War
1 Taxes had increased/trade had been lost/there was a great war debt.
2 1928.

90 Industrial conflict
1 Having one 'employer' to bargain with/being able to get national as opposed to local wage rates.
2 When the government gave a subsidy to the mine owners to prevent wage cuts in 1925.
3 The Organisation for the Maintenance of Supplies – it recruited volunteers to help break the expected strike when the subsidy ran out in 1926.

91 Ireland
1 Eamon de Valera.
2 Because some were opposed to accepting the partition of Ireland.

92 The Depression
1 The collapse of the US stock market.
2 Cuts in unemployment and sickness benefits, and in the salaries of public employees.

93 Formation of the National Government
1 The Conservatives.
2 Most were against, and became the Opposition.

94 The National Government in action
1 The Conservatives.
2 It introduced the 'means test'.

95 Recruitment
1 Essential/skilled workers were needed to maintain war production.
2 Help resist the expected German invasion.

96 Propaganda and censorship
1 The Censorship Bureau.
2 It kept back bad news and exaggerated successes.

97 The Battle of Britain
1 It gave the factories – and the RAF – time, at a critical point, to replace the planes that had been lost.
2 That the number of German planes destroyed was exaggerated at the time.

98 The Blitz
1 ARP wardens.
2 May 1941.
3 (i) Flying bombs (ii) rockets.

99 Evacuation and rationing
1 The lack of attacks led them to think it was safe to do so.
2 January 1940.

100 The role of women
1 Single women, aged 19–30.
2 This was the only organisation that gave women the same training as men, and allowed them to take part in military combat.

Answers

www.bbc.co.uk/revision